C000042971

Crisis Management

Jack Gottschalk

OPERATIONS

06.05

■ Fast track route to understanding crisis management

■ Covers the key areas of crisis management from crisis planning and handling a global business crisis to crisis plan execution

■ Examples and lessons from some of the world's most successful businesses, including Parsons Corporation, Pepsi Cola, Johnson and Johnson and General Motors, and ideas from the smartest thinkers, including Douglas Hearle, James E Lukaszewski and Fraser P Seitel

■ Includes a glossary of key concepts and a comprehensive resources guide

>>EXPRESS EXEC.COM<<
essential management thinking at your fingertips

First published 2002 by
Capstone Publishing (a Wiley company)
8 Newtec Place
Magdalen Road
Oxford OX4 1RE
United Kingdom
http://www.capstoneideas.com

CIP catalogue records for this book are available from the British Library and the US Library of Congress

ISBN 1-84112-215-7

Printed and bound in Great Britain

This book is printed on acid-free paper

Contents

Introduction to ExpressExec

ExpressExec is 3 million words of the latest management thinking compiled into 10 modules. Each module contains 10 individual titles forming a comprehensive resource of current business practice written by leading practitioners in their field. From brand management to balanced scorecard, ExpressExec enables you to grasp the key concepts behind each subject and implement the theory immediately. Each of the 100 titles is available in print and electronic formats.

Through the ExpressExec.com Website you will discover that you can access the complete resource in a number of ways:

» printed books or e-books;
» e-content - PDF or XML (for licensed syndication) adding value to an intranet or Internet site;
» a corporate e-learning/knowledge management solution providing a cost-effective platform for developing skills and sharing knowledge within an organization;
» bespoke delivery - tailored solutions to solve your need.

Why not visit www.expressexec.com and register for free key management briefings, a monthly newsletter and interactive skills checklists. Share your ideas about ExpressExec and your thoughts about business today.

Please contact elound@wiley-capstone.co.uk for more information.

Introduction

A description of the need for crisis management in the public and private sectors, and in both the for-profit and not-for-profit areas.

"Great crises produce great men and great deeds of courage."
John F. Kennedy

Why is crisis management important? Simply put, without it, and without a plan to accomplish necessary goals, crises grow and relationships are damaged in the long term, short term, or both. And no organization is immune. Private sector for-profit companies can lose customers, while not-for-profit groups can lose credibility and members. Governments, too, can suffer. Agencies can have trouble getting funding having once lost the confidence of the executive or the legislative branches. Elected officials can lose their jobs the next time that the voters go to the polls.

In short, when something goes wrong, no matter who is at fault and regardless of the reason, someone must tell the story as quickly as possible. Will there be a "spin" on that story that will make the organization look good? Probably. But that's not necessarily bad as long as there aren't lies and deliberate distortions that will come back to haunt the organization later.

If an organization has just had a disaster that killed and injured a lot of people or poisoned the environment, there will be no question that the incident happened. When any organization talks about its plans for taking care of victims and to help make things right, that's a good thing. If that's considered to be putting a "spin" on a story, so be it. Ducking the issue or letting the media or the government tell the public about a crisis or its underlying causes is never a good idea.

The future is, of course, here. We live more, every day, in a global society that is increasingly held together by a complex system of linked and rapid communications. When the oil tanker goes onto the rocks in Alaska, or when a plant explodes in India, or when an airliner crashes into Long Island Sound, the world media knows about it with lightning speed. The world learns about the incident only minutes later. And both the media and the public will be impatiently waiting for accurate information, including explanations for the event, immediately.

The task of meeting that challenge falls to the people who plan, and are responsible for carrying out, effective crisis management operations. Particularly in the US, the media and the general public take the "right to know" as an article of faith. It can safely be assumed that this desire will be increasingly observed around the world as capitalism and associated democratic government inexorably spread. Thus, the need to be ready to communicate when things go wrong, to engage in crisis management, will continue to be an ever-increasing part of management's responsibility during the twenty-first century.

What is Crisis Management?

What the terms used really mean and how to understand the differences between them.

The first problem, when dealing with the various definitions of crisis management, is to understand what the activity really is, and who are the people engaged in it.

One definition, albeit not the only one that has been offered to describe an imprecise activity, has been provided by Larry Smith, president of the Kentucky-based Institute for Crisis Management. His view is that a crisis of the type dealt with in this book is:

> "A significant business disruption which stimulates extensive news media coverage. The resulting public scrutiny will affect the organization's normal operations and also could have a political, legal, financial, and governmental impact on its business."

CRISIS ACTION PLANNING

In one sense, particularly at the highest levels of government, crisis management can easily be viewed as creating tactics to deal with a fast-developing situation with national security ramifications. The people who make their living dealing with such things have essentially given this kind of problem-solving an official date of creation – October 1962. The occasion of its birth was the Cuban Missile Crisis and the group involved in the crisis management was the Kennedy White House.

Academics and government officials have come to label this activity "crisis action planning," but it is sometimes given a shortened title of "crisis management," a fact that does have a definite tendency to confuse.

EMERGENCY PLANNING

The term "crisis management" is also used, incorrectly as far as the purpose of this book is concerned, to describe those activities that involve what must be done before and during some kind of emergency. Thus, when the factory catches fire, the efforts to ensure that the workers can escape and that the blaze can be extinguished, are often thrown into the over-arching term of crisis management as opposed to what it really is in such a case, namely "emergency management."

Another example reinforces the distinction between crisis management and emergency management. When the lights go out in the accounting department for a few hours on pay-day, that's an emergency which quite clearly causes great inconvenience, but, when plant number three in North Carolina, or Rome, or Caracas, explodes with a deafening roar and pushes some horrible chemical five miles up into the sky for all the world – and the media – to see, that's a crisis that can imperil the very survival of an organization.

DIFFERENCES AND MYTHS

What sets crisis management, in a public relations sense, apart from both crisis action planning and emergency management is its media aspects. There is a recognized need to inform the public about the problem, generally through the news media, how it is being handled, why it happened, and how it will affect people.

There is not, by the way, any real belief on the part of crisis management consultants or executives that what they do will result in the public learning to love their organization. People do not like any organization, regardless of what it is, any better when it is honest with them. When, for example, PepsiCo proved that it wasn't responsible for insulin syringes turning up in some cans of its products, or when Gerber proved that there was no way it could have put glass in baby food, customers did not lovingly embrace the corporate entities involved.

And that's okay, because the real driving motivation behind crisis management efforts is not to make people love a company or any other kind of organization. The idea is to reach out to the various critical publics – the media, customers, financial community, shareholders, government – and not have them like the entity any less.

Anyone who says that crisis management, regardless of how effective it proves to be, will help an organization to be cuddled by society, has been living in a cave for a very long time.

PUBLIC RELATIONS, CRISIS, AND THE NEWS MEDIA

The root of crisis management, again using the term in the sense being discussed in this book, comes from the skills that have been honed over the years by consultants and executives in the communications and public relations field. For the truth is that no matter how one tries to look at this activity, unless an organization reaches the biggest number of people possible with its version of events during a crisis, the crisis management effort fails. And the only real way, in the vast majority of situations, to reach a lot of people fast, is through the news media via the reporters and editors who make that system work.

Obviously, paid advertising can be, has been, and is, used to reach people. When the tire issue involving Firestone went into high gear, Ford Motor Company featured its CEO in a series of TV ads. He talked about how Ford was both determined and dedicated to having safe tires on its vehicles. There is at least some anecdotal evidence to suggest that a news story in *The New York Times* would have carried more credibility than the words of a Ford executive, but that is an arguable issue.

On the same point, and dealing with the same crisis, the new CEO of Firestone was also featured on TV ads attempting to convince viewers that "when the rubber hits the road" it will remain on the tires. Only time will tell if these crisis management, public relations-oriented efforts, generated from a huge crisis, will prove successful.

A rule of crisis management, of course, is that people must be informed and that such communication be accomplished before somebody else, for example, the government, does it. There is no doubt that when any organization reaches out to the public to tell its story, it will try to do it without making a bad situation worse. And so it has come to pass that the media and others have created labels for application to the communicating public relations consultants, executives, lawyers, and anyone else involved in getting a story out. The labels run from the mildly offensive to the downright corrosive, including "spin masters," "spin doctors," and "flacks."

The real point is that when things go wrong, somebody has to do something. And there is nothing wrong with an organization trying to inform the public with its version of a disaster and with the greatest extent of honesty and truth that can be provided. No organization, private or public sector, can afford not to communicate, and not to do it with skill. In a crisis, silence is not golden.

Evolution of Crisis Management

How crisis management has developed, using selected crises of modern history to illustrate successes and failures.

There have always been disasters of the character that, today, would trigger crisis management efforts. Among them, during the twentieth century, would be: the sinking of the *Titanic* in 1912; the Teapot Dome scandal of the 1920s; and the widespread labor troubles that plagued America during the years immediately following World War II.

A list of the number of incidents over the years would be a long one. They have involved organizations and individuals, and they have been marked by one interesting thing – there was *no* crisis management, certainly of the type practiced today.

Certainly, there was a desire on the part of affected organizations, such as the New York Stock Exchange, National City Bank, White Star Line, and Sinclair Oil, to avoid or limit damage to corporate interests caused by newspaper headlines. And there were, without question, discussions between executives and newspaper publishers and editors that may have helped in that regard.

But there is no real evidence to show that organizations faced with disaster took steps that were based on any crisis plan, or tried to get to the news media ahead of the story with a less damaging and perhaps helpful version of events.

THEN AND NOW

Public relations, though at the time of its earliest use it was not blessed with a name, has its roots in the need to communicate with large groups of people and to try to win them to a cause. The Greeks and, to a greater extent, the Romans, used communication techniques to rally the masses. The Roman Catholic Church was an early master in the use of mass communication to "propagate" the faith, a term that led to the word "propaganda," which, in reality, is what public relations is all about.

The availability of printing put a lot of wheels under the communication process, giving anyone with access to a press the means to reach huge numbers. This ability also created substantial problems for established government and led to attempts at censorship because of the (correctly assumed) fear that when people have a lot of information they can be harder to control.

This fact, of course, was no better proved than in the days of colonial America when a number of people, among them Samuel Adams, began to raise hell with the established order. When the Civil War started, Thomas Paine, a pamphlet writer in the employ of Washington's army, did his bit to push the soldiers and the general population (a substantial percentage of whom were either loyal to the British Crown or didn't particularly care about who won) into a patriotic fervor.

Business, however, tended to ignore the use of mass communication as a means of winning the hearts and minds of the masses until well into the second industrial revolution, which began after the end of the Civil War.

It cannot be said that the media of the time ignored business. As John Steele Gordon, in his book *The Scarlet Woman of Wall Street*, noted as one example, a *New York Times* editorial of November 19, 1868, dealing with the Erie railroad scandal, which read:

> "England and France have had their speculative bubbles, their gross violations of trust, their robbery of confiding stockholders by men high in position, and with riches in abundance. But neither England nor France presents a parallel to the infamies of the Erie railroad."

The fact, of course, was that no major corporation or business leader was going to be damaged by a negative press. It was, truly, the era, as one of the Vanderbilts said in anger to an inquiring reporter, in which business could and did take the position that "the public be damned."

But that was to change as government and the media began confronting big business interests that were, by the turn of the twentieth century, being considered as a national threat. As a bigger government, armed with bigger regulatory teeth, a president (Theodore Roosevelt) armed with a big stick, and investigative writers took aim at business leaders, they realized that something had to be done to make them appear to be warm and cuddly. Ivy Lee, probably the nation's first real public relations professional, told the media that he would provide about and on behalf of his clients: "prompt and accurate information concerning subjects which are of value and interest to the public . . ."

It is, of course, extremely difficult to pluck an event from history and then place it into a modern frame of reference for purposes of comparison. But, it might work here and in any event, we'll try.

If, on a dark and stormy night in the fall of 1932, a fully-loaded oil tanker had collided with some rocks off Alaska, or bounced off a sand bar in the Gulf of Mexico, with the result that thousands of furry little seals were drowned in the oil slick, there would not have been a crisis. The story might have been reported (and perhaps not) but few people would have cared. And no one would have seen the furry creatures or the oil-soaked birds flapping in the black water.

In the same vein, while there was an understandably high level of patriotic interest in how well we were doing during World War II, there were no pictures of dead US soldiers released to American audiences until 1943.

Another example, perhaps apocryphal but relevant, is the oft-related story of two military officers who showed up right after a twin-engine bomber hit the 79th floor of the Empire State Building on Saturday, July 28, 1945. One said to the other: "What shall we tell the press?" The senior officer replied: "Deny everything."

Whether that story is true or not, another example is a matter of fact. During the dark days of the Cold War, the US government did have a plan that called for national press censorship in the event of emergency. And there was a manual on how to conduct it. One of the rules was that if there was an atomic attack on the US, the news should not be released to the media.

The currently, and widely, recognized need to open and maintain communication channels with the public took a while to gain acceptance. Even today, as will be seen, a lot of organizations are not committed to the idea. If it were not for the fact of lightning-fast and multiple types of telecommunication, most organizations, instead of only some, would still avoid having to inform. It's not in most organizations' genes.

Remember that delay of getting pictures of dead soldiers into the hands of the American public in World War II? Compare that with the endless TV shots of body bags that were visited upon Americans in their living rooms during most of the years of the conflict in Vietnam.

By the 1950s, the American public expected to be kept informed about most things. The newspapers were fewer in number and they were giving way to the immediacy of radio. And by the 1970s, television had mounted the throne as king of journalism. It would stay there, with the change being in the form of networks to some extent being replaced by, for example, CNN.

Government had to learn to live with these changes and, to some extent, it did that better than the private sector. Generally, public relations people in government are news sources and they meet with the media on a continuing basis. They have long ago learned how to "leak" information, conduct "deep background" briefings, how to hold news conferences, and how to make and maintain news media contacts.

Practice doesn't always make perfect, but it helps. The private sector has a different set of problems and, to a large extent, significantly less experience. Most companies, even the biggest of them, are not sources of real news. They do try to be and they are always ready to issue publicity releases on people who are getting promoted, what new products or services are being offered, and how good the profits are, particularly the after-tax ones. A relatively small amount of this information gets into the newspapers except for the business journals and far less gets onto the TV screens.

TEXAS CITY

But the private sector was not ignorant of the need to communicate in a disaster; at least that was true of some companies. The first crisis management plans were in place at least as early as the late 1940s and were created by some of the major banks, chemical companies, and airlines.

One grim day in April 1947 brought the example that proved the need for crisis communication. Texas City, Texas, was the place. A ship blew up in the harbor and that explosion caused massive fires and more explosions at the nearby Monsanto Chemical plant and in several oil refineries, one of which was operated by Humble Oil, a part of Standard Oil Company. The resulting destruction and loss of life made national headlines. If there were crisis plans in place, there is scant evidence of their effective use.

But there are far worse cases that can be used as examples of poor crisis management or a downright corporate lack of interest in communicating to the public.

"LOVE CANAL"

Once upon a time, for those who cannot remember, there was a toxic dump near Niagara Falls, NY, that was used and abused by Hooker Chemicals & Plastics Corp. from 1947 to 1952. After its complete contamination of the site, Hooker sold the poisoned ground to the Niagara Falls Board of Education in 1953. As late as 1992, Hooker and its successor company, Occidental Petroleum, didn't want to talk about the site, which came to be well known by the name "Love Canal."

Would Hooker have been better off in the eyes of just about everyone if it had accepted responsibility for the use as a toxic sewer? Sure. But it didn't. Did it matter? Ask the people at Occidental.

A LITTLE BENZENE

Perrier, well-known for its expensive little green bottles of water, took cover when benzene was found in some of those containers in 1990. Did it hurt Perrier? Maybe, for a little while. Most people forgot the whole thing anyway.

THE TWA CRASH

When TransWorld Airlines (TWA) had a plane go down into the waters off Long Island a few years ago, it was roundly (and wrongly) criticized by some people in the media because it did not immediately release the names of the passengers on the manifest. The airline took the position that it had to check the manifest to be sure it was correct and then it had to reach family members before giving that list to the media.

And then TWA held a news conference that had to be one of the greatest crisis management disasters on record. It was done live in a hangar and conducted by airline executives who seemed to have no concept of how to deal with the media in a crisis atmosphere.

Did the handling of the disaster hurt TWA? Maybe, but if the company was damaged, there were other causes. There is a point to be remembered. Maybe Occidental wasn't hurt by Love Canal. People still order Perrier water. People still buy TWA airline tickets.

But if there is another major disaster involving any of these companies and it doesn't get its story out to the public via the news media fast, the reporters and the editors will be reminding the public of what happened before.

DOING IT RIGHT

But there are good examples of dealing with the public in a crisis as well as bad ones. Johnson & Johnson and the Tylenol poisonings, and Gerber Products Company, Inc. and the allegations of glass in its baby food, are illustrations of how to do things right. Both cases will be more fully examined later.

The Tylenol case, of course, stands out as one of the first product-tampering crises and Johnson & Johnson gained a permanent position as a pioneer in dealing with that sort of problem. It took the product off the retail shelves, it talked to the media, and it communicated with customers, and other target groups.

Gerber took similar action when confronted with false claims about glass in its baby food. But it did not take the product off the shelves because, had it done so, corporate financial disaster could have followed.

Both companies knew what they were doing and what they had to do to survive these crises. Again, they were not loved by the public but they did survive and prospered.

The key point is that if the management of any organization refuses, for any reason, to talk about its people, products, or services, or about any problems that can affect the public, it runs a very real risk of not being trusted at all. That is the reason for effective crisis management.

A time-line follows showing some key incidents and dates. Several of the noted incidents will be presented as case histories in Chapter 7.

TIME-LINE

- » **1947**: Texas City explosion and fire. A major disaster with seemingly minimal crisis management involvement.
- » **1979**: Three Mile Island. Too many people trying to talk to the media with resulting confusion. One individual must be designated as the spokesperson in a crisis.
- » **1982**: The Tylenol product-tampering. A milestone case with a company, Johnson & Johnson, doing virtually all things right.

» **1989**: The *Exxon Valdez* oil-spillage disaster. Confusion and lack of information in the midst of chaos. Exxon spent a lot of time, energy, and money to prove, before the crisis, how responsible and open it was. And then the ship, literally, hit the rocks.
» **1996**: Parsons Corporation loses its CEO in a widely reported plane crash. Its planning for such news and its execution of the plan are excellent examples.
» **1999**: Crisis management insurance cover is made available.

The E-Dimension

How new means of communication have impacted crisis management in terms of challenges and responses.

There are several parts of this subject which apply not only to crisis management but also to the entire area of mass communication.

Clearly, one of the first considerations is that news, good or bad, travels with frightening speed. What this can mean is that a company with far-flung operations may easily be placed in a position of not having enough advance notice to be able to respond to a story about itself. If the concept of trying to get out in front of a story is a viable one, the practical fact is that it may be harder to accomplish now than it was only 10 years ago.

The ability of the news media to cover stories and to get the story out around the region, nation, and world, has also been enhanced by the use of e-mail, faxes, cell-phones, and the computer. One example of how these inter-linked technologies have changed things is to examine the news coverage of American military actions in a combat zone in a modern sense.

THE MILITARY GIVES UP

In virtually every conflict involving American military forces since the end of the Mexican War of 1848, except for Vietnam and it was considered there, military news from the front was subject to censorship. The telegraph lines were monitored during the Civil War, and there was naval censorship of the cables sent by the press from Key West, Florida, New York City, and Washington, DC, during the Spanish–American War. The media was also censored by the military during the US intervention in Vera Cruz in 1914. Censorship of the press was conducted in France during World War I and in every theater of operations during World War II and, later, in Korea.

But by the time of the Gulf War, the idea of censoring a correspondent's material was so difficult to accomplish that the entire censorship organization, known as the military's Wartime Information Security Program (WISP), was abandoned. It was replaced by a far more loosely-organized news management system that worked only because the war was so short.

Why the change? There was no way to effectively censor, no matter how important that might be, given the electronic resources that were available to the news media, including private communication satellites.

IT'S NOT JUST SPEED

But it's not only speed and better communication tools that make the e-dimension an area of concern to the folks in crisis management, it's also the potential (and the reality) that now exists to attack any organization and do it in a public forum. The attackers, current or potential, are out there in cyberspace.

In its April 12, 1999 issue, *Business Week*, in an article entitled "A Site for Sore Heads," explored the problem of "e-attacks" that must now be confronted. One example was that of an unhappy customer of a Wal-Mart store. So unhappy, in fact, was the customer that he created walmartsucks.com. This Website platform, according to the magazine, has been used by a lot of people (some 1500 customers and employees) to file complaints and other communications against the company. Of course, not everybody can take a joke and Wal-Mart went to its lawyers for an answer. The lawyers, of course, threatened action and the Website operator basically told them to get lost. In an apparent attempt to make something positive out of the whole thing, a Wal-Mart executive told *Business Week*, after backing-off in trying to shut down walmartsucks.com, that: "we are not going to get into a tit-for-tat with people on the Internet."

And this is just one incident. Many, if not most, of America's largest companies, from airlines to banks, brokerage houses, and retailers of just about everything, have become the targets of unfriendly Websites. United Airlines, for example, has had to deal with its name being changed to "Untied Airlines" on a Website that was designed to help people file, and get faster results from, complaints.

Another example of becoming a target is IKEA, the furniture retailer. Apparently, at least one Website was used to send off complaints about the way in which IKEA did business. Now, of course, there is nothing wrong with complaining about any business and the use of a Website may well be the modern equivalent of letters via snail mail, which required fireproof gloves to hold while reading them.

Other major companies that have found themselves on the receiving end of Website complainers include Chase Manhattan, Nike, Radio Shack, and Dunkin' Donuts. The list, of course, is only a sampling and gets longer every day.

The concern in the new century is that complaints made on the Internet are very, very public. And, unlike the old days, when occasionally an irate customer bought newspaper space or rented a billboard to send a message, the Website user incurs no cost.

Even with that, most organizations understand that valid complaints are a good thing and they are encouraged on the Internet or by any other way. Obviously, of course, it is one thing to deal with people whose complaints are valid and to try to make things right. It's another when attacks are unmotivated and have been designed to damage.

BEAT 'EM OR JOIN 'EM

So, what is an organization to do? There appear to be several options available but there is a lot of debate on which one, or combination of them, is the best choice.

The first option, and probably the best one (if it works), is for the organization under cyberspace attack to follow one old and proven tactic that simply involves making contact, defining the problem, and finding a solution. Maybe that irate Website complainer has a real problem and somebody, a retail clerk, a store manager, a credit supervisor, a bank teller, or a manager, screwed up.

In our modern society there are ever-increasing numbers of people who believe, often justifiably, that big government and big companies don't give a damn about them. The Internet is a great place to vent frustrations. Some people will, of course, vent more than others.

The first option may be a long shot but, if successful, the pay-off can be substantial.

A second option when dealing with Websites is for a company to create its own. Modern companies, after all, are supposed to be good at communications. This is a great test of that alleged competence. A favorite defense seems to be to buy up Websites that have their name on them with either the words "ihate" in front of, or "sucks" after, their name. It's a tactic that's certainly less expensive than going to court.

And here's a thought on that possibility of dealing with unhappy people on the Internet. If a company or other organization has made a mistake, why not go public with an apology? It's a cardinal rule in crisis communication that a company should seek and seize every opportunity to tell its story. What better way than to use the Internet to counter bad news?

A third recommended option when dealing with Website complainers is to take the action that some companies have selected. When faced with Internet complainers who don't have real problems, they identify the negative Websites and then offer to buy them. Apparently this method is also considered to be more cost-effective than litigation.

Two obvious problems arise: first, there is the potential charge that a company is effectively paying out "hush money;" and secondly, it seems to ignore the creativity of those who zoom around in cyberspace. It's not hard to put together a Website. If Joe knows that Peggy got paid to stop annoying a company, he might set up a site so that he will get some dough too.

Lastly, an option when faced with the need to stop the Internet complainers is to fall back on the time-honored American position: SUE THE BASTARDS! The lawyers, of course, like this tactic, at least if they're litigators. But there is one large problem with unleashing the lawyers to get the Internet rascals. It's called the First Amendment. The courts and the lawyers are wrestling with that part of the Constitution and how it works in the cyberspace environment. While the legal community debates the finer points, the Websites proliferate.

And that's a tough old bird, the First Amendment. Remember, the founding fathers thought that freedom of speech was important enough to be put at the top of the Bill of Rights.

Of course, most companies and other organizations that find themselves targets of Website complainers are pretty big. In many, if not most, cases the Websites could just be considered an annoyance that will eventually go away. In fact, that is yet another option, not doing anything.

However, if a company or organization is not a large one and is unfortunate enough to find itself a Website target for reasons that it cannot change, the results can be total disaster. Today, that possibility has to come with the risk and the cost of doing business.

CRISIS AND SHAREHOLDER IMPLICATIONS

And what about, specifically, crisis management and the e-dimension?

At least up to this point, no sudden disaster has occurred that might give cyberspace warriors the chance to make a bad situation worse. Examples of what could happen include e-mail or other e-dimension attacks during a developing crisis that might take the shape of rumors, possibly designed to create panic. The potential for creating havoc in such supercharged situations as Three Mile Island, Bhopal, the Tylenol scare, and other product-tampering cases, is obvious.

Another corporate issue arising from the application of modern technology specifically represented by the Web, is the input of unhappy, and possibly organized, shareholders on a corporate board. From well back in the mists of corporate history, there were always some people who predictably showed up at annual meetings armed with one share of stock and were determined to have their views heard and to generally raise hell.

Sometimes, very rarely, the protests were valid. In most cases, the complaining shareholders were on hand to promote some personal or political agenda. They did what they did, however, in a semi-private setting. Now, of course, the attacks and the complaints can be made and continued from a Website and, to resurrect a phrase from the 1960s: the whole world is watching.

BEST PRACTICE

There is a good possibility that companies engaged in the retailing business are going to be more vulnerable to, and as a result will feel more threatened by, Website complainers than, for example, the banks and insurance companies, which seem, historically, to be somewhat less sensitive to public unhappiness and complaints, real or not. Retail customers, after all, have a well-known reputation for being fickle.

So, the chosen example of best practice in dealing with a crisis comes out of the fast food portion of the retail maze. The company is Dunkin' Donuts Inc., and, according to the April 12, 1999 issue of *Business Week*, when the famous retailer was named by an unhappy Website complainer who had created dunkindonuts.org., it not only offered to buy the site from its creator, it also provided coupons for free donuts to people who had sent in complaints. As a spokesperson for Dunkin' Donuts Inc. told *Business Week*: "If this was where customers were going to post their complaints, we thought it was important for us to go ahead and address them."

That's called excellent customer awareness as well as being a terrific example of how to create a positive from a negative.

The Global Dimension

An examination of what organizations should be prepared to do when facing international crisis incidents.

There are some serious considerations to deal with when discussing globalization and its application to crisis management, or perhaps the correct way to phrase it is the application of crisis management to globalization.

Most large companies, both foreign and domestic, are engaged in global business in the true sense of that term, which is that they operate facilities of some kind beyond their own borders. And most of these companies, surely most American ones, have crisis management plans in place.

But, as already mentioned, there is a major difference between planning and execution. It is that latter part of crisis management that is extremely difficult to do well when a company tries to tell its story beyond the shores of the US. And that will be particularly difficult to accomplish in the developing countries around the world. Never bet on the attempt being successful. If you do, get points.

In most cases, the salvation is that American companies should and will expend most of their efforts targeting publics that are, for the most part, here. And so, when the American manufacturer of a whizz-bang, high-powered chemical toilet bowl cleaner gets the unhappy news that lightning has just made its plant in Faisalabad a red-hot pile of hissing poisonous gas, the US executives will be wishing that the factory was somewhere in New Jersey.

The harsh truth is that crisis communication, which is supposed to get the best and, presumably, the most honest version of a disaster out quickly to the concerned public, can't work in most of the world. Why? Because most of the world can't understand the message and won't believe it if it did. Plants explode, airliners crash, factories burn, and people die all around the globe, every day. Crisis management does not have an equal vitality everywhere that such disasters occur.

The key to effective crisis management, or at least one of them, is to know the groups to be targeted with information. If one of a US airline's planes crashes in the middle of the jungle in Burma, the primary target audience isn't there. It's in the US because that's where the company "lives."

If a plant owned, whether or not operated, by a US company blows up and sends a greenish-purple haze in the direction of downtown Khartoum, the primary target audience is still essentially here in the

US, although it would expand to include the host country's national government, the media, and through that media, the affected populace.

KEY LEARNING POINTS

» There are three key points to remember when dealing with crisis management and its global application. The first is to clearly understand how the crisis can hurt the organization. The second is to identify the target groups that hold the levers of power that may control public opinion in any foreign environment. The third is to understand how best to reach those groups.

» The cultural, economic, and political considerations that are inherently part of crisis management beyond the borders of the US are vitally important and are often ignored. There is a tendency to believe that everyone around the world thinks about things in the same way as does the American public, or the majority of it.

» In many parts of the world, public relations and crisis management are considered as essential government tools that are used to tell the public how it should vote, how it should react, and how it should behave.

» Even in countries that are friendly to American interests, political leaders are quick to jump on an anti-American theme if that will demonstrate to the masses how those leaders can stand up to US power. Very often, and increasingly, that power is represented by the presence of American business.

BHOPAL IN SHORTHAND

One good example, perhaps the best one to have yet taken place in terms of an international crisis and a specific US company, involved United Carbide and Bhopal, India, in 1984. While the case is used at the end of this chapter as a best practice example and is presented in greater detail, an overview of it is given here.

Union Carbide, which was not unsophisticated in the use of PR, the employment of crisis management, and the problems of doing international business, could not do much during this crisis to reach the people of India either directly or through the media. The emotions of the hour ran high and the Indian government helped to raise the level of intensity.

The US media was faced with the need to make a choice between what Union Carbide said had happened at Bhopal and the version set out by the Indian government. The latter source was determined to make a bad situation only look worse and make the whole thing the fault of the US company. Indeed, the management consulting firm of Arthur D. Little, in a report on the Bhopal tragedy, noted:

> "In the immediate aftermath of a large-magnitude incident, both non-technical and technically-trained reporters converge on the site, looking for quick 'answers' to the question of what caused the event. Most reporters are responsible, restrained, and unbiased in their reporting. However, a fringe group usually appears on-site that is more interested in developing causation theories, which seem to have great public appeal, regardless of their veracity."

Compare this short version of the story with the three key points set out above. There was knowledge of what could happen in such a plant and what would be the result in terms of damage to the company. Given what happened and how, there was little the company could do to make things better in India. The people who held the levers of power were all inside the highly nationalistic foreign government. Given that, the Indian media supported the government position. There was, as a result, no effective way to reach the people of India with the truth as it was being delivered by Union Carbide. The only group that could be reached, and the most important one, was the US public, and so Union Carbide spent most of its efforts in communicating to its shareholders, the media, and the public in the US, while at the same time recognizing that it could not ignore India or the rest of the world.

But most of what it said outside of the US fell on deaf ears. Look at it this way, a lot of people find business dull. Most people do not read the financial pages and if there is a down-and-dirty choice to be made between perusing the sports coverage in the *New York Daily News* or the headlines of the *Wall Street Journal*, the sports guys win by a mile.

What this means is that a lot of people, even in the US, had never heard of Union Carbide, much less about Bhopal. There is even a very good chance that a lot of Americans have no real idea where India is on the map. If the most important target group is going to be hard to reach, it's going to be much more difficult, even if the foreign nation and its media are helpful, to be heard somewhere over the rainbow.

And then you add the foreign bias. People in Khartoum (or pick a place) are going to get the news of what is happening in their country via a filter that will probably not be pro-American and almost surely not pro-American business. When those previously mentioned fumes over Khartoum are shown on local TV there, the voice-over comments will fairly glisten with dripping venom.

The people here, the shareholders and the US government, will, as a result, always represent the primary target audiences for crisis communication. Presumably, a US company knows, if it has done its job of crisis management planning, how to reach those groups with maximum effect.

As part of the process of getting out there ahead of the developing story, a company can and should provide information as best it can on what happened and why; what the company is going to do to help make things better, and what contacts have been made in the foreign country. All of these points have a major news value.

Obviously, Union Carbide could not control the actions or the attitudes that were exhibited by the Indian government. The difficulty in that case was that Bhopal became not only an industrial disaster but also a potential international crisis. The only course of action in that kind of a scenario is for the company involved to make contact with Washington and to work with federal officials to keep things reasonably calm.

The Bhopal case was probably summed up best in a statement made by one of the attorneys who represented Union Carbide when he said:

> ''There were three tragedies at Bhopal – the gas leak, the reaction to it by the Indian government, and the consequent inability to get relief to the genuine victims.''

The final advantage of going to the Feds (and of doing it fast and publicly) is to dump the problem in the laps of those people who are paid with tax money to deal with friendly, hostile, and neutral nations.

Essentially, then, successful handling of a crisis that takes place in a foreign country is far more difficult than doing the same thing at home. It's a matter of degree, with a lot of faith being placed in planning and having well-trained people around to execute the program.

The crisis management plan should contain a foreign disaster contingency, but the principal focus must be on the US target groups.

BEST PRACTICE – UNION CARBIDE IN BHOPAL

Union Carbide's classic foreign crisis took place on December 3, 1984 at Bhopal, India. The company operated a pesticide production facility there and, on that day, a large quantity of methyl isocyanate gas was released into the air.

The incident took place during the early hours of the morning and caught a great many Bhopal residents asleep in their shanties and shacks. By dawn the gas had cleared away, but it had already caused deaths and injuries resulting from inhalation of the toxic fumes. In the end, possibly helped by some creative Indian government accounting methods, there were claims of some 3800 dead and 11,000 injured in one way or another.

News of the disaster, which the Indian government immediately blamed on Union Carbide, was received in the US almost 12 hours after the gas had escaped. The first reports were, as expected, fragmentary. But there was enough information for the highest executive levels at Union Carbide to begin working on what had to be done.

From the outset, corporate executives knew that the Bhopal incident was a serious one. First, there were the continuing reports of deaths and injuries. Second, there was the knowledge that any company in the chemical business was always at risk of a disaster. Third, if something went wrong in a foreign country, the US owners of the plant were probably going to be faulted even when they weren't responsible.

Union Carbide began the process of crisis management by holding a news conference near its headquarters in Connecticut. It provided facts about the production process and the use of methyl isocyanate, told the media that it was sending medical supplies and experts to the site, and announced that it was beginning an investigation into the disaster.

The information provided at the news conference was communicated to both the Indian government and the Indian media, as well as to the US and all foreign news agencies. Additionally, the company position and its action steps were communicated to its employees around the world, and to shareholders and other critical target groups. As a clear signal of its concern, Union Carbide immediately closed down production at a West Virginia facility that used the same chemical and manufacturing process as that at Bhopal. The plant would stay closed until the Bhopal investigation was concluded.

Despite the company's good faith attempts to conduct the investigation, there were road-blocks set up by the Indian government, particularly as it began to appear that at least one (and perhaps more than one) Indian worker with grievances not against Union Carbide but against the Indian government, had sabotaged the plant.

Meanwhile, the Indian government fanned the flames of controversy and increased the level of anti-Union Carbide rhetoric, all designed to shift public focus away from the anti-government motives of the perpetrators.

While this case is a complex one that is obviously given here in a shortened form, the main point is clear. The company did everything it could do and communicated to everyone who would listen. But even the most well-planned, best-intentioned, and best-executed crisis management program will have difficulty when it is expected to work in a hostile foreign environment.

The State of the Art

How the field of crisis management is organized, the types of experts who are in it, what they do, and where they fit into organizational structures.

The father, if you will, of crisis management, is public relations. The overwhelming number of experts in the field of crisis management come from that discipline.

This fact in itself creates some problems and issues. Public relations is a "soft" management activity, as compared to marketing for example. The marketing executives take pride in being able to show, through numbers and charts, how their function directly impacts sales of relevant products and services. In most charts, the heads of marketing, finance, and operations (or manufacturing, depending on the business) are on an equal level and part of the general staff.

The public relations chief, in most companies, is a member of the special staff and, as such, reports directly to the chief executive officer, president, or whatever the particular company has titled its biggest cheese. But, historically, the public relations person has been highly expendable and usually the length of time spent in jobs is short. By comparison, marketing executives last much longer.

ANOTHER COMPARISON

Even that special staff position is interesting when taking note that the corporate legal counsel is also usually a special staff member. As a result, a look at a lot of corporate organization charts would lead to the mistaken belief that the public relations and legal executives have the same status within the management hierarchy. But, of course, that is hardly true.

A real difference is that top management may disagree with its lawyers on some issue of major importance but it's a good bet that they won't disregard that professional advice. The public relations function does not have, and never will have, such a status within the business community. In short, public relations experts, whatever their training and expertise, are not trusted to the same extent as their lawyer counterparts.

There are some good reasons for this. Lawyers have been around longer; they have statutes and case precedents to back up their views; a knowledge of how laws and regulations apply in a specific situation; and they are paid to keep an organization out of the kind of trouble that can be measured in money. Finally, lawyers are recognized, licensed professionals with required academic credentials and strong bar associations at the local, county, state, and national levels to look after their interests.

The people down the hall, in the public relations office, have to keep selling themselves to top management and, when functioning as independent counsel, they have to keep promoting the value of their services to current and potential clients. There is, as a result, a large reservoir of insecurity and feeling of inferiority in the public relations ranks that has not seen any marked reduction over the passage of time.

Now, these points about how public relations and the people in that field feel and are viewed (and, by the way, they are often former journalists and some are lawyers) are transferred to what they do when a crisis management situation develops. Most organizations have elected to use public relations for crisis management planning and its execution when the proverbial balloon goes up. However, a lot of top management types do not feel terribly comfortable about the selection and, in recent years, some have retained general management consulting firms to put together the plans.

When it gets to the execution, public relations people, because of their knowledge of the news media, will still have an edge in the same way as they do when sending out news releases. And there is the previously noted inability of the public relations activity to demonstrate its effectiveness by some objective measure. In an age where everything gets measured by numbers, this is damning. It used to be that public relations tried to show its value by showing top managements and clients scrapbooks of news articles. Of course, that doesn't really tell anyone how much of the material was read, understood, believed, or, if desired, acted upon.

Taken a step further, how can an organization know it's better off than it was in the eyes of Wall Street, its industry, competitors, or any other target group with which it is concerned? The answer, of course, is that it can't.

And when the business community takes a long, hard look at some crises of the past (*Exxon Valdez* stands out as a major example), it will ask whether crisis management, good or bad, really mattered in the long run. Sure, the price of Exxon shares went down on the New York Stock Exchange when people saw the TV shots of dead, oil-soaked seals and birds. And yes, a lot of gasoline credit cards were sent to Houston. But, in the long term, did Exxon or the oil industry in general get hurt? The answer is no.

Did TWA really lose out in the air competition wars because of the fact that it handled the initial phases of crisis management like a botched abortion? Maybe. But who can tell?

Despite these points, and the obvious associated uncertainties, there is no denying that crisis management planning and execution is a growth activity. The media and the public have come to expect an organization to say something when a disaster occurs. Still, not every large organization is prepared to do that. No crisis plan exists for the same reason that a lot of people don't have a will. The inevitable will never happen. Then . . . it does.

ENTER THE INSURANCE POLICY

And so, to make the crisis management process easier for companies that find themselves with a need for it, insurance became available.

The idea of having insurance coverage to pay some of the costs incurred by a company in its belated efforts to restore or maintain its image during a crisis is not really a new one. It was the subject of some, at least, informal discussions as far back as the 1960s.

But the pioneer that introduced the first policy and is thus accorded that distinction is the National Union Fire Insurance Company. As initially available, the policy would provide up to $50,000 to cover the cost of hiring an approved crisis management consultant.

The insurance policy set out the names of several well-known consulting firms that had to be used by a company in the event of a crisis. It was interesting that not all of the listed firms were in the public relations business. One, for example, was engaged in private security and investigations work.

Currently, AIG Excess Casualty Company provides coverage under what it calls a crisis communications policy. AIG is a division of American International Companies, the largest insurance carrier in the field of business insurance and one of the largest in the world in terms of international business. Its crisis communications coverage is designed to help a company get through an event that could severely damage not only property but reputation.

According to information provided by the insurance carrier, the claims process begins when the insured notifies the company that a crisis has taken place. The notification must be made, according to the company, by a "key executive." The carrier's Website information states that:

> "This is an event that could result in a claim seeking damages that will exceed the limits of underlying insurance or the insured's self-insured retention and lead to high profile negative media attention."

The insurance provides an amount up to $250,000 to cover damages claims made as a result of a crisis. In addition, AIG's crisis funding policy can provide up to $50,000 to pay for crisis management consulting services.

COMMUNICATING VALUES

Another issue that arises regarding crisis management planning and execution is how well an organization is thought of before some awful event happens.

The tough question is whether or not anybody really cares about the values of, for example, an airline when the bodies of passengers are being dragged out of a snake- and alligator-infested swamp or fished from the ocean. Do people really listen to an oil company's much-trumpeted pronouncements about how it worries about the environment when baby seals are dying in a thick ooze created from the hemorrhage of a tanker that hit a rock? The answer is: probably not. But it's that nasty little word "probably" that, if nothing else, creates the need for crisis management.

Corporate income, to include sales, and what can happen on Wall Street, are in the mix. There can be no doubt that taking effective crisis management action is better than taking the chance on not doing anything.

If there was proof that there would be no damage sustained by an organization when a crisis occurred, few firms would spend the time and money needed to plan for one. But they don't know. And so, crisis management, which does benefit the public, is forced on most companies as a requirement of doing business.

However, when the crisis hits, the need to talk about values is as important as giving out information about the crisis itself. It's part of an organization's credibility and, important as it is, communicating the values message is sometimes ignored in the haze and inevitable confusion of developing disaster.

A "VALUES" QUIZ

Organizations, no matter what they are or what they do, can't just talk about their values, they have to prove them. Like going on a diet, it can't hurt to start today.

What do the critical target audiences think about the company? Do the employees really like working there? Does the company have a good relationship with suppliers? Does the rest of the industry look upon the company as a leader? As a quality competitor? Do customers care? Is the company in a business where customer loyalty is important? Does the mission statement, that is so proudly hailed in the annual statement, truly reflect the organization's beliefs?

While all of this sounds terribly basic, it is equally terribly important. When the crisis hits, even the media, which is almost always cynical, will (sometimes) tend to listen with less suspicion when a company has proven to be honest in the past. One example, an old one, but good, will prove this point.

During the 1970s oil crisis, while motorists were impatiently sitting in long lines, often in the pre-dawn darkness, a lot of big oil tankers were riding at anchor in Lower New York Bay near the refineries. All of the ships were low in the water. One did not have to be an admiral to know that they were loaded with something. Presumably, since they were oil tankers, they were not carrying tomato juice.

The news media, in particular the television part of it, were very interested in those tankers. They flew over them every day and persistently raised the possibility that just maybe there was oil in the boats and it was going to stay there until the price of gas went up at the pump. There was never any satisfactory answer to what was in the tankers. And then the crisis ended, everybody could get gas, and the tanker questions were no longer news.

One day, about a year later, New York University held a seminar for public relations executives on radio and television news and the media. One of the panel members was from an oil company and he talked about effective public relations and winning the hearts and minds of the media. In one of the rows toward the back of the room sat an assignment editor for one of the TV flagship channels in New York. He was becoming increasingly and obviously annoyed as the oil presentation droned on.

And then the time came for Q&A. In a tone that had the same level of friendliness that is associated with the rattle of an angry diamondback, he asked: "Why didn't you guys answer our telephone calls about the tankers in the Narrows?" There was a long silence. And then someone chuckled and the moderator got off the subject and let the oil spokesperson off the hook.

A few years later, the *Exxon Valdez* hit the rocks off Alaska. No matter what Exxon could have done in that crisis, they would have had an uphill fight trying to convince the American media that they were telling the truth.

The moral is clear. Companies that want to get the most out of crisis management efforts must have established values and have communicated them before, not just during, a disaster.

ANOTHER VIEW

Making the point again, Dr Laura Nash, in an article for the summer 1995 issue of *The Public Relations Strategist*, wrote:

> "Certain patterns dominate the seasoned cynic's skepticism of seemingly well-intentioned corporate values and vision programs. The first is the perception of hypocrisy. Most frequent comment: 'Yeah. This all looks good, but it's the way management walks that really counts. They've changed the talk, but they're still walking the same way.' Clearly, any significant reality gap between corporate culture and a values statement will not go unpunished."

What all this tells any organization is clear. It has to mean what it says regarding organizational values and it has to show those values over and over again, not just when some crisis occurs and the company wants to be thought of as a really nice place to work for or do business with.

And, getting back for a moment to the cold waters off Alaska, did Exxon really worry about what anyone in the world cared or thought about it when its then chairman, Lawrence G. Rawl, waited for 22 days to visit the site of the *Valdez* disaster? The gas was selling well at the pumps and Wall Street didn't care (then or now) about the furry little seals.

MEDIA AND BIAS

While efforts have been made here to take the reader through the salient portions of crisis management planning and the pitfalls of execution, one thing is still missing. How the news media operates and what it wants are things that are necessary to know. But does there exist an anti-business bias on the part of the media? Another, more cynical, way to phrase the question is, of course: how biased against business is the media? The answers for the most part are "yes" to the former and "a lot" to the latter.

There is no real debate when the majority of public relations executives are asked about it. They feel (and most people in the media admit) that journalism, in both the print and electronic forms, is inhabited mostly by political liberals. The idea is that business is out to screw the world and that the only force that will keep that from happening is, of course, them. In all honesty, the media also believes, liberal or not, that government is also in the screwing business and that it too must be brought to heel before the power of the pen, camera, and microphone. The bias of the media is constant. It does not simply surface when there is a crisis. It just becomes more evident at those times.

Since the long ago days of the early twentieth century, "muckrakers'" business has been a target and there were often good reasons for it that go beyond such obvious points as illegal price-fixing, sweatshops, monopolistic practices, and the like.

In large measure, business people, even today, only talk when they want good news to be read and heard. Despite all of the media training that is available, when executives think that the media has latched on to something negative, many will still fall back on "no comment" as a knee-jerk response.

Another reason is that business, except when there is a crisis involving it, is not going to be page one news or make the top of the TV news hour. As noted earlier, most business news is pretty dull and that's true for editors and reporters as well as for viewers and readers. Face the facts, most reporters would much rather cover a crisis that involves a riot or a factory fire than have to attend a shareholders' meeting, or a product roll-out, or hear about how some corporation has decided to donate money to the homeless.

Now, of course, there are those reporters and editors who make their living covering business. But the total number of such journalists is very small in comparison to the others in the field. And when there is a disaster, the first reporters on the scene and the first editors who will get the information from them, or who may be frustrated in their attempts, are general assignment people. You can take it to the bank that the more frustrated they are, the more anti-business they will become.

BIASED? PROVE IT!

It is, of course, difficult to prove bias on the part of the news media because there is always the answer, on its part, that it is either not understood in terms of serving the needs of the public or, taking a more belligerent stance, that it doesn't have to respond at all.

Remember the famous comment by Edward R. Murrow, who was once asked about the thin skin of the media whenever it was criticized. He replied to the effect that the media was not thin-skinned – it had no skin at all.

And the media can show its bias, or its independence, in a lot of ways. There is no question that poor old Spiro Agnew was right when he said that the mere voice inflection of a national newscaster can send whatever message that journalist desires. For those who might doubt that statement, it is very strongly suggested that they try to honestly monitor the broadcast news and the print media.

Headline writers can achieve the same ends. If an editor wants to deliver one message in a headline about, for example, the efforts of a company CEO to offer aid to victims of a disaster, the headline can read: "Jones Will Offer Some Help to Victims." A more friendly set of words would be: "Jones Offers Assistance to Victims."

A reader of the first headline could easily infer that Jones is a certified SOB who is going to send as little as possible to those poor suffering victims. The second headline gives the impression that Jones is really interested in getting something done in the midst of disaster.

ANTI-GOVERNMENT, TOO

People in government, from the White House to thousands of town and village halls across America, at least sometimes have the same unhappy feelings about the media. Sometimes it is even more anti-government than it is anti-business. There is a difference, though, and it is one that gives an edge to the government.

As was noted earlier, most government agencies are a continuing source of news to the media. Few companies really are. It is also true that because government officials are a source of news, even their complaints about the media will appear in print or be heard on the air. It is more of a fair fight. Obviously, when the private sector tries to engage in that kind of a battle, it is generally doomed to make bad things even worse. It is another part of crisis management that comes with the territory.

A LOOK TO THE FUTURE

A lot of things can happen to companies and to other kinds of organizations, but there is one essential fact that cannot be ignored. There will always be plane crashes, train wrecks, fires, explosions, chemical spills, financial scandals, and a whole bunch of other miserable events that will bring massive unhappiness to the executive offices.

The good news is that more and more American organizations are preparing to deal with crisis through the preparation of plans. The problem, of course, as we have often seen before (and will see again), is that the execution of crisis plans can leave a whole lot to be desired.

Another problem is that, as companies become more and more involved as players in the international arena, there will be an increasing need for them to learn more about foreign cultures, ways of doing business, and how the news media operates in faraway places.

Ultimately, as with any planning process, the results will generally be somewhat different than what is desired. Executives will say the wrong things, the media may be hostile, the disaster may be of such a nature and magnitude that organizational credibility may be impossible to achieve. There are no guarantees, just best efforts.

In Practice

A presentation of case examples showing how crisis management has been successful and where it has either not been used or failed.

Public relations and its crisis management component are both relatively new management skills. The result is that there is, compared to law for example, a rather limited accumulated experience.

One helpful thing that does exist to help guide both lawyers and public relations executives and consultants is the existence of cases. Lawyers, of course, use cases in a far more organized and systemized manner. They're largely taught through the use of cases which represent and illustrate what has been decided in the courts. Public relations people use cases as examples of how well (or how badly) things have been handled and that, of course, includes incidents of crisis management.

Another essential difference is that most cases referred to by lawyers, law professors, and judges are reported ones – that is, they have been published. The legal profession also uses unreported cases, those decided but not published, but both reported and unreported cases are part of a public record.

The cases that public relations people use as examples are those that deal with large issues: plane crashes, tanker spills, explosions, corporate financial scandals, and so forth. These cases are known because of the disaster and its reporting by the news media. A lot of other crisis management problems involve small organizations and don't get much, if any, media attention. And there are some incidents which do get media coverage but where the affected organization does not talk about the internal operations of its crisis plan.

And so, given all of these caveats, some of the most useful cases are older ones where what happened was either public from the beginning or has become so with the passage of time. Despite their seniority, cases like those discussed below have a continuing value in the study of crisis management.

Having set the stage with far too many words, the cases that will be examined here involve: Firestone and the infamous tires; Coca-Cola and the adulterated soda; General Motors and its conflict with NBC; Parsons Corporation and the loss of its CEO in a plane crash; Pepsi-Cola and the insulin syringes; Jack-in-the-Box and the bad meat; Gerber and the claims of glass in its baby food; PanAm and Lockerbie; Johnson & Johnson and the Extra Strength Tylenol recall; and, finally, the burning cruise liner, *Sun Vista*, and its boatload of unhappy passengers.

FIRESTONE AND FORD

The unhappy connection between Firestone, which makes tires, and Ford, which makes Explorer trucks, is well known. The case, however, can only be subjected to limited examination because not all of the facts are available. In addition, what the long-term effects may be on either or both companies is impossible to reasonably predict. As of this writing, both companies, as might be expected, are blaming each other.

It is known that there were problems with the Firestone tires as far back as 1996, when KPRC, a Houston, Texas television station ran a piece about them. It is also known that, until the story emerged of how a lot of accidents had happened, with associated fatalities and injuries, neither the appropriate federal agency, the National Highway Traffic Safety Administration (NHTSA), nor Firestone took any action. And then there were the claims made by Firestone employees that quality was not a big concern back at the tire factory.

Finally, there was the recall of millions of tires, a belated statement by Bridgestone/Firestone (Firestone's parent), and then television ads that featured the top executives of both companies. The main message was that Firestone and Ford were dedicated to putting out a quality product with safety as a paramount concern.

Meanwhile, the tires were returned, the scope of the original recall was expanded, Ford and Firestone continued to blame each other, Congress held hearings, and, of course, the inevitable lawsuits were filed by and on behalf of those who were killed and injured when the infamous tires peeled off.

The death-toll finally reached 174, in addition to over 700 injuries and more than 60,000 complaints about such things as tire separations and blowouts. And, of course, in terms of international public relations, there have been a number of deaths in the Middle East and in Venezuela that were allegedly connected to the faulty tires or to the unhappy tendency of the Ford Explorer to roll over, or both.

Lawsuits number in the hundreds, with both Ford and Bridgestone/Firestone obviously expecting the worst. A clue to that is the fact that Ford has already stated that damages being sought by claimants have reached some $590mn and that Bridgestone/Firestone is looking at an estimated $750mn in costs, which include the huge tire recall.

The number of tires pulled off the shelves came to 6.5 million and there are demands by some consumer groups that the number be increased to 16.5 million and the recall be expanded to include additional types.

KEY LEARNING POINT

Despite the recent vintage of the case, there is at least one valuable point that was proved once again. Any organization that is really interested in doing a credible crisis management job must be prepared to talk to the media and the public quickly. If it doesn't tell its story, someone – the media, the plaintiffs' lawyers, the government, or all of them – will.

The interesting question, which as yet remains unresolved, is whether the public, and in particular the tire- and vehicle-buying parts of it, will believe either company. An even bigger question is whether the public will care, perhaps believing, as it seems to do with politicians, that big companies lie all the time and there isn't anything that can be done about it.

COCA-COLA AND EUROPE

Sometimes, despite a company's experience and obvious skills in marketing, merchandising, and promotion, the ball gets dropped on the goal line when it comes to a crisis. The Coca-Cola Company, and its handling of its 1999 crisis in Belgium and France, is one great example.

The world's most popular soft drink was gulped down by a couple of hundred people, including children, all of whom were on a vacation tour. Something in the drink that had, by accident, gotten into the bottles made a lot of them sick.

Coca-Cola, which should have known better, did not get ahead of the story. The media in both the US and Europe ran stories about the incident but, apparently, Coca-Cola just read them.

Finally, after 10 days of media coverage, then Coca-Cola CEO, Douglas Ivester, flew to Europe and made a belated appearance to explain what had happened.

KEY LEARNING POINT

The damage, of course, was already done. Whether the problem was the result of accident (as it turned out to be) or whether it had been from any other cause, there should have been a more aggressive crisis management action on the part of the company. Organizations under siege must respond quickly if they truly believe that crisis management is important.

GENERAL MOTORS AND NBC

The essence of crisis management, the principal reason for the time, money, and effort that goes into what is hoped will be success, is getting the organization's message out to the public through the gatekeepers of public information, the news media.

Sometimes, of course, there can be those extremely dark days when the crisis is *caused* by the media. General Motors had to deal with that task in November 1992 when NBC ran a documentary on its TV magazine format program *Dateline*, which alleged that at least some type of General Motors trucks were inherently dangerous.

NBC didn't just make the claim, it ran a video that showed how a General Motors truck would explode when hit by a car. It was a convincing piece of evidence in support of the allegation. It was, it turned out, also set up.

General Motors had to take action. It was the subject of a serious attack on part of its core business and the assault took place in front of a lot of viewers, somewhere between 17 million and 20 million of them. Even if it wanted to, General Motors could neither run nor hide. The die was cast.

General Motors did its crisis management job right. It demanded an apology along with an explanation from NBC, while it conducted its own investigation into how the crash depicted on TV was done, where, and by whom.

The investigators got lucky. But, as it is sometimes said, luck is better than being good. In this case, there was both luck and skill. A firefighter who had been on the scene when the staged accident took place and had shot a videotape of the event came forward to talk about it.

And that was just the beginning. General Motors found the trucks that had been used in the NBC piece. One of them contained evidence which indicated that some kind of incendiary device, specifically a model rocket engine, may have been used.

Throughout all of this, and over a period of several months, General Motors sent numerous letters to NBC regarding the piece. There was no response. NBC was hanging tough. And then General Motors filed suit. And the General Motors engineers were busy demonstrating that what was shown in the NBC program couldn't have happened without some artificial help.

The General Motors crisis communications campaign was a well-orchestrated one that included, along with the engineers, a highly-developed media relations effort. At the same time that the lawsuit was filed in February 1993, a two-hour news conference was held in which the offending tape was shown to the reporters in attendance. The effect on the NBC position was, mildly put, devastating. The next day, February 9, 1993, NBC broadcast a public apology to General Motors.

The combined and well-orchestrated efforts of General Motors's lawyers, engineers, and public relations executives, along with a consistent position voiced by top management that the company had been wrongfully attacked, worked. NBC would wind up with a lot of egg on its corporate face, and some people there got fired.

In a report issued in late March 1993, an internal NBC memo noted in part: "... it is a story of a breakdown in the system for correction and compliance that every organization, including a news organization and network, needs."

One might say, of course, that the word "including" could have been replaced by the word "particularly."

KEY LEARNING POINT

The questions, of course, are obvious. Did the rigged story create another crisis, namely one at NBC? The answer is yes. Did it hurt the network in viewership or advertising revenues? The answer is no. If NBC had made the same false claims against some company that did not have General Motors's resources, what would have been the result? The answer is that a smaller company could have been destroyed along with innocent employees and shareholders. The public probably would have believed any major news organization that made such a claim. People will tend to believe the media's version of events more than one offered by most "profit-driven" companies, not-for-profit organizations, and the government. The fact that news organizations are also in a profit-making activity is usually lost to public perception.

PARSONS CORPORATION

Disaster can come in a number of ways. Some of them are totally beyond the ability of an organization to predict. The sudden, traumatic loss of a senior executive is a good example of such an event.

In April 1996, the Parsons Corporation, a Pasadena, California-based engineering and construction company, was suddenly hit by the news that its board chairman and CEO, Leonard J. Pieroni, had been killed in a plane crash, which also claimed the life of then Secretary of Commerce Ron Brown.

Parsons, a company that is owned by its employees, acted swiftly, not only to replace Pieroni, but to keep the company operating smoothly while showing respect for the Pieroni family and keeping employees informed.

The key to the installation of a new executive to head the company and to keep the business moving along was due to planning. As *Business Week* reported in its April 22, 1996 article on the incident:

"The employee-owned company's by-laws specify that the president has all the duties and responsibilities of the CEO in his absence. And they spell out the procedure that provides for succession."

KEY LEARNING POINT

Many companies that are otherwise considered as well managed have not set up that kind of crisis provision. In the event of a similar incident, the picture presented to employees, the media, and the rest of a company's important target groups, can be one of confusion, if not chaos.

PEPSI-COLA AND THE SYRINGES

This is one case where a company that was, and is, highly sophisticated in the area of crisis management, broke one of the cardinal rules of the discipline and got away with it. The company did not get ahead of the story.

It all began on June 10, 1993 when someone in the town of Fircrest, Washington, claimed the discovery of a syringe inside a sealed can of Diet Pepsi. The next day another syringe was alleged to have been found in another can of the same soda but in Tacoma, Washington. The cans were said to have been sealed and both of the syringes were of the type used by diabetics to administer insulin.

The local media found out about the cans and the syringes and the story quickly found its way onto the Associated Press wires and into print and broadcast stories around the nation. And then, to loosely coin a phrase, the fit hit the cans.

The syringes became national news, but Pepsi-Cola said nothing, and this was initially thought, at least by some, to mean that this was an in-plant sabotage. Another theory that surfaced, given the diabetic connection, was that the syringes might possibly have gotten into the cans by accident during the production process. Either way, it was going to be mighty bad news.

The Food and Drug Administration (FDA), which takes a dim view of things like syringes in soda cans, started getting restless, largely because of the growing media coverage. Pepsi, meanwhile, despite the silence, was on the move behind the scenes. First, while it was virtually certain that the syringes could not, either by accident or design, have gotten into the cans during the manufacturing process, it was going to be absolutely sure. There was no room for error and Pepsi knew it. Second, the company was getting ready to go public.

The problem was a growing one of public confidence. When Pepsi said nothing to immediately defend itself or to take some kind of action, there was the growing belief that it had something to hide. The media was being joined by consumer groups that now were trotting out that magic word "recall" – the expected product-tampering tactic that had first been used by Johnson & Johnson during the Extra Strength Tylenol crisis. But Diet Pepsi was a much more critical product to the overall corporate profit picture than Extra Strength Tylenol was to Johnson & Johnson. Simply, the pharmaceutical manufacturer could afford to recall its product. If Pepsi did that with its product, the final result could be crippling in terms of lost market share.

Things got worse when the FDA started giving out warnings to the public in the north-western states, plus Alaska, Hawaii, and Guam, to check all Diet Pepsi cans for possible tampering. The FDA warning, combined with the national media coverage, inevitably opened the doors for publicity seekers and nutcases around the country. People were claiming to have found syringes in Diet Pepsi cans in virtually every state and territory. And then somebody was arrested for slipping a syringe into a can. The apprehension was made in Pennsylvania and only five days after the first report had been made in Fircrest.

Pepsi-Cola's crisis communications program clicked into high gear. Pepsi executives appeared on TV talk-shows and on the news. Updated information, including a store surveillance videotape showing the person trying to get a syringe into a can, was sent to all the media.

The personal appearances were backed up by three video news releases (VNRs) that were used to show the Pepsi production facilities and the company's attention to safety and anti-tampering measures, as well as to illustrate the company's packaging. Finally, one of the VNRs contained a store surveillance videotape that showed the customer trying to insert a syringe into a Diet Pepsi can.

All during the crisis, Pepsi kept its employees fully informed of its actions, the belief (correctly) being that the company's employees were a critical target audience for the Pepsi message. And Pepsi reached out for help from an independent third party, the FDA, whose chairman, Dr David A. Kessler, appeared with Pepsi's CEO, Craig Weatherup, on national TV in support of the company's innocence and co-operation.

When the crisis was over, Pepsi ran several full-page ads in the national media which, essentially, thanked the public for their faith in the company and its product.

KEY LEARNING POINT

It took guts for Pepsi to hold off making a public announcement until it was fully ready to do it. It showed a lot of internal confidence in the safety of the company's production process. And it paid off. The dip in sales of Diet Pepsi that had occurred during the syringe crisis was more than offset by the increase that took place in the months following the tampering incidents.

JACK-IN-THE-BOX AND THE BAD MEAT

This company, operating fast food outlets, principally in the Pacific north-west, was shaken badly by an outbreak of food poisoning that came from hamburgers eaten by many of its customers during January 1993.

There were a lot of sick stomachs, some 800 of them. Included in that number were 3 deaths and 144 people who were admitted to hospital. One child died as a direct result of the bad meat. The first thing that the company did, quite naturally, was to stop selling hamburgers in the area from which the complaints had originated.

Several days after the first reports of sickness had been received, and as more came in, the president of Jack-in-the-Box, Robert Nugent, appeared at a company news conference held in Seattle. He offered his hopes that everyone who had gotten sick from the hamburgers would recover and admitted that the problem lay in contaminated meat.

The company tried to get ahead of the story with the admission that the meat was bad. But its contention that there was no fault on the part of Jack-in-the-Box was shaky from the start. One problem was that the company had been charged by the Washington State Health Department of being in violation of established safety and healthy-cooking procedures, regardless of whether or not the meat was contaminated.

It was the company's claim that a meat supplier provided the contaminated beef and that the State of Washington, which had charged the company with violating its health regulations, hadn't told Jack-in-the-Box about the recent changes in those state-established regulations. Specifically, Nugent said to the assembled media:

"While the Washington State Health Department recently, and we think appropriately, upgraded their temperature regulations for hamburgers, it is clear that Jack-in-the-Box was not properly informed of this change."

As things turned out, that statement was untrue and Jack-in-the-Box would pay the price for it.

No government agency, at any level, is going to become the bad guy in this kind of a situation and, if there was ever one thing to remember about bureaucrats, they do tend to keep records. True to the statement, the people in the Washington State Health Department had theirs.

And so, as they say, it came to pass that when the annual meeting of Jack-in-the-Box was held some weeks later, and when the bad meat stories were rapidly fading from the front pages, Nugent was forced to make a damaging admission. The new regulations had, in fact, been received and were on file both at the company's home office and in the Tacoma, Washington site where the offending hamburgers were cooked.

The end result was, indeed, a dismal one. The value of the company's shares fell like stones off a cliff and the lawsuits against Jack-in-the-Box multiplied. Faced with the effects of two crises, the first involving the bad meat and the second in giving out what proved to be false information about the receipt of health department regulations, Jack-in-the-Box did what it could in terms of damage control.

It settled the lawsuits, a good tactic whenever possible since court battles generally mean even greater and, from the point of view of a corporation versus a consumer, negative news coverage. Jack-in-the-Box also engaged in a major program, through media advertising and distributed literature, to inform the public about what it was doing to make things right for the victims and their families. One key element of the campaign was the statement by Robert Nugent who said:

"We are committed to meeting all of our responsibilities in connection with this devastating situation. We are prepared to pay all hospital costs for our customers who have been affected by this tragedy."

KEY LEARNING POINT

Despite efforts to pay the hospital bills of the affected customers and a campaign of advertising designed to rebuild its customer base, Food Maker Inc., the Jack-in-the-Box corporate parent, suffered badly in the eyes of its shareholders and the public in general. When a company gets ahead of a developing story in a crisis, it must have all the facts. Food Maker didn't.

GERBER AND THE GLASS

Glass pieces in baby food? The allegation was loud and totally without basis in truth. Sometimes, too often, as in both the Pepsi-Cola and Gerber cases, the truth gets lost in the media glare and the consumer advocacy frenzy.

The first report about the glass came from up-state New York in February 1986 where a woman said she had found glass in a jar of the company's baby food. Upon learning of the claim, Gerber obtained the jar and others bearing the same product identification code and rushed all of them to the company's lab for testing. The New York State Health Department did the same analysis at the same time.

And then the media jumped in, at one time reportedly asking shoppers if they knew that the baby food might be contaminated with glass. And that was enough for some government leaders who just might have had their own obvious agendas. The Brooklyn, New York District Attorney talked about a possible criminal investigation and the governor of Maryland ordered Gerber's strained peaches off retail shelves in that state.

Gerber took the position that *it* was the victim and acted accordingly. As both its own tests and those of everyone else showed the baby food to be without any trace of glass, the company moved forward. It launched a major media blitz that included both the local and national news outlets; it responded to every media inquiry about every complaint; it reached out to consumers in its advertising and via mailings; and it asked for, and got, support from the FDA about its production safety procedures.

Not only were the media, the government, and customers targeted by the company, so were the retailers who stocked Gerber products, shareholders, and employees. Full, continuous communication, specifically tailored to meet the needs of the company's publics, was critical.

> ## KEY LEARNING POINT
> The results of the efforts were highly positive, a point best illustrated by a rise in product market-share over the level that existed before the crisis.

PANAM AND LOCKERBIE

The terrorist bombing that blew PanAm Flight 103 out of the sky over Lockerbie, Scotland, on the night of December 21, 1988, resulted in the deaths of 270 people and effectively ended the corporate history of the original PanAmerican World Airways.

The story of the bombing itself has become a major part of history, with much wider applications that involve geopolitics, international tensions, and the workings of international justice. But the case has also generated important points for consideration by people who are interested in, and responsible for, crisis management in a more limited sense. Given the nature, the inherent drama, and the sickening aspects of the unnecessary tragedy, it is vital to examine what the airline did and did not do in the hours and days that followed the crash.

The airline's first word of the crash was received from wire-service reporters and the only available confirmation was that the plane had dropped off the radar screens. Soon afterwards, PanAm was able to confirm the crash, as did the Federal Aviation Administration (FAA), although the first reports as to the number of passengers and the cause of the disaster were incorrect.

At the beginning of the crisis, the airline took steps that it should have taken, including setting up a dedicated telephone line for the relatives and friends of those who were known to have been aboard the downed plane. As part of the company's well-designed crisis plan, teams of PanAm employees were created to deal with the anguish of those who had lost loved ones. The company's offices in the PanAmerican building in New York were sealed off to permit effective crisis management operations. And then the airline went public to discuss the aircraft, a 747 Boeing jet, how it was built, specifics of its maintenance record, and its proven structural soundness.

The first news conference was held in the early evening at the PanAm offices. By that time, the correct passenger (and thus fatality) count was available and given to the assembled media. As required by the company's standard operating procedures, no names of passengers were divulged pending notification of the next of kin.

Despite being pushed by reporters as to the cause of the crash, PanAm spokesman Jeff Kriendler refused to speculate on that point despite the growing feeling that there was something more than a tragic crash involved. In fact, less than an hour after the plane went down, experts in the US and the UK knew that the crash was caused by an act of terrorism.

The initial handling of the crisis on the part of PanAm has to be considered as excellent. The well-designed and rehearsed crisis plan that had been developed by the airline functioned well. But there would prove to be a problem that the crisis managers could not control.

The day after the crash, the news media learned that several weeks earlier, the FAA had advised a number of government agencies that an anonymous threat had been received by the American embassy in Helsinki, Finland, that a PanAm flight from Frankfurt en route to the US would be bombed. While it was later shown that the threat had no connection to the actual bombing, the fact that the airline had not warned its passengers became another public relations problem.

From a historical view it is interesting to compare the firestorm reaction of the families of victims in this case to the far more restrained one that occurred after the liner *Lusitania* was sunk by a German U-boat in 1915. There is a close similarity, based on the warning posted by the German embassy in New York before the ship sailed that it was considered to be a legitimate target. Cunard, the ship's owner, did nothing affirmatively to warn passengers, about 1200 of whom died off the Irish coast.

Several weeks later, PanAm CEO Thomas Plaskett flew to the UK to attend a memorial service for the victims of the bombing. Despite that, there was criticism from the public about the fact that he had not flown to the crash site immediately after the disaster. There was also a continuing chorus of criticism from people who claimed that PanAm should have told passengers about the threats that had been received by the US government in the days before the bombing.

> ## KEY LEARNING POINT
>
> Despite all of the things that PanAm did right during the crisis, the incident was clearly one of several factors that put the carrier out of business. Because of these other reasons, which were essentially financial, the full impact of the incident and the long-term effectiveness of the crisis management actions that were taken, will never be known. When an incident occurs that is totally beyond the ability of an organization to prevent, and when there are other major factors in the mix, including financial performance, effective crisis management may not be enough to keep the company going as a viable entity. Without such management, however, its demise is virtually guaranteed.

THE EXTRA STRENGTH TYLENOL POISONINGS

There is probably no debate about the fact that this case is the one most remembered and cited by crisis management consultants, executives, and academics. The essential facts are well known. In late September and early October 1982, six people died as a result of swallowing Extra Strength Tylenol capsules that contained cyanide. Extra Strength Tylenol was a major product marketed by Johnson & Johnson, a highly respected company with headquarters in New Jersey.

An investigation into the deaths, led by the Federal Bureau of Investigation, began with the full co-operation of the company. It was clear from the beginning that the cyanide used in the murders had not been placed in the capsules at the company's facilities, although one early problem occurred when the company first stated that it didn't use cyanide in any manufacturing process. The company was forced to correct that statement – a fact that caused some temporary loss of corporate credibility.

Despite that knowledge, Johnson & Johnson took the capsules off the market and sent warning letters to hospitals, doctors, and pharmacists about the problem. In addition, all product advertising was immediately halted.

The point person for the company in this crisis was its chairman, James E. Burke, who earned much-deserved credit for his actions and personal leadership. Burke ordered the worldwide recall of Extra Strength Tylenol at a cost to the company of roughly $100mn. He authorized a $100,000 reward for the arrest and conviction of the killer and supervised a program that offered to exchange money for capsules that were in the hands of consumers. Finally, he ordered a major communications effort, using both advertising and publicity, to calm the public and to retain the confidence of customers and other target groups.

One important part of the Johnson & Johnson program was to have a national opinion survey conducted. The point of the survey was to determine the public's view about Tylenol and thus to assess the level of damage that had been sustained as a result of the crisis. The results were disturbing. According to the survey, approximately 87% of the people queried believed that the company had no responsibility for the cyanide incident. On the other hand, 61% said they would not buy the product.

The position of the company was set out by Burke, who said: "It is our job at Johnson & Johnson to ensure the survival of Tylenol and we are pledged to do this." A new tamper-resistant package for the product was designed and introduced. But tamper-resistant is not tamper-proof. By the end of 1982 the company's market-share had been largely restored but corporate happiness was to be short-lived.

In February 1986 another fatality was reported and, once again, the capsules were taken from the shelves. This time the cost was estimated to be $150mn. The capsules were then taken out of production and replaced with caplets. At that time a much disappointed Burke noted: "I'm heartsick. We didn't believe it could happen again and nobody else did either."

The end of the cyanide crisis and its handling by Johnson & Johnson marked the establishment of Burke as a modern corporate hero who received the compliments of no less than President Ronald Reagan who told him: "You have our deepest appreciation for living up to the highest ideals of corporate responsibility and grace under pressure."

KEY LEARNING POINT

Despite the huge costs incurred in two crises, the tactics used by Johnson & Johnson paid off in long-term profits and target group confidence. Johnson & Johnson took the kind of action that its huge resources permitted it to take. Extra Strength Tylenol was one of many over-the-counter medications marketed by the company and while there were heavy financial costs, the company could (and did) successfully absorb them. Another important fact was that, as in the later cases of product-tampering involving Gerber and Pepsi-Cola, Johnson & Johnson was confident in the integrity of its manufacturing process. Finally, the need to get out ahead of the story was again demonstrated.

SUN VISTA SAILS INTO TROUBLE

Most of the passengers aboard this 30,000-ton cruise ship in May 1999 probably believed that ocean liners didn't burn and sink except in the movies. They do now. The *Sun Vista* did catch fire and sink. And it took their personal belongings with it. In all, there were 1104 people, including passengers and crew, aboard the 8-decked ship when it caught fire while steaming off the coast of Malaysia.

While it can be expected that people might lose baggage when their ship catches fire and disappears beneath the waves, there were serious allegations that Sun Cruises, the company operating the liner, did very little to make the tired, dirty, and, yes, scared, passengers feel better.

Some of the passengers said that they were not given the company-promised hotel rooms in Singapore. Others complained that the company failed to help them by providing enough cash. A number of people said that they lost all of their clothes, money, credit cards, and jewelry when the ship went down.

In what has to be considered in the history of crisis communications as one of the great understatements, the cruise liner's spokesperson told the media: "We didn't expect them to all come off smiling."

When the company president appeared on television in Singapore, he took the position that the ship had been on fire for several hours before the need was determined to abandon it. Contrary to his statements that the evacuation was done without panic, passengers said that panic ruled and that they were given no information as to the ship's status. Finally, they were put into lifeboats and were in the water for up to 12 hours before being rescued.

The fact that no passengers died in the smoke, flames, or water very quickly moved the story from the front page of most US newspapers to inside the front section – a point that was a public relations blessing for Sun Cruises.

KEY LEARNING POINT

Whether the company had a crisis management plan, or whether it was used, is unknown. The main point is that any company that moves people around on land, at sea, or in the air must pay close attention to crisis. The potential for disaster is both high and imminent.

Key Concepts and Thinkers

Some views about crisis management as provided by three of the most well-known and highly-respected professionals in the field.

The views of well-regarded professionals should always be given a lot of attention. In the related fields of public relations and crisis management there are a lot of people whose credentials are suspect. This unpleasant fact generates all kinds of heated debate within the ranks of those engaged in the disciplines.

And so, in this forum, readers should consider themselves highly fortunate to encounter the views on several subjects related to crisis management as offered by three of the field's most respected practitioners: Douglas Hearle, James E. Lukaszewski, and Fraser P. Seitel. Brief biographies are given with each of their presentations.

DOUGLAS HEARLE

We begin with *Hearle's F-words*. Douglas Hearle is a senior consultant in the area of special and crisis situations. He is a former president and CEO of Carl Byoir & Associates and was chairman of Hill and Knowlton Inc.

HEARLE'S F-WORDS – DOUGLAS HEARLE, SENIOR CONSULTANT

Over more than three-and-a-half decades of working in the field of crisis communication, I have learned that there are no rules appropriate to all situations – save one. That one is: never forget that every crisis involves people and therefore every communication in a crisis must address the human factor.

With this in mind, it becomes obvious that the management of communications during a crisis must resonate with human emotions, human values, and human experiences. Crisis resolution ultimately will be measured by the achievement of relief – a human emotion.

In order to keep myself on track in managing a crisis situation, I developed a series of what I termed my "F-words." I'm sure with the help of *Roget*, I could have found these reminders under other letters of the alphabet, but since crises usually involve *frustration*, I arbitrarily chose the letter F. Besides, the term "F-words" has a certain panache.

If your program addresses all of the F-words, it will succeed. If it does not address them all – omits even one – it will fail, because it will be judged in human terms. Here they are.

» **FAST** – whenever possible be the **FIRST** to bring a crisis situation to the attention of your publics. If you are the wellspring of information right from the beginning, you will have a greater degree of control. The fact that you make the **FIRST** announcement will also earn you some goodwill credit which you might very well be glad to have.

» **FULLY** – don't hold back. Provide as much detail as possible. Picking and choosing information, especially information that ultimately will come out, will erode your credibility later on. The more information you are able to provide, the fewer questions others will ask and the less speculation will occur. This helps keep you in control.

» **FACTUAL** – be as specific as you can. Don't communicate in generalities. There's a practical reason for this. **FACTS** are the ultimate truth. **FACTS** do not change, so you won't find yourself "backing and filling" later on with phrases like "what we meant to convey . . ." and "we didn't mean to suggest . . ."

» **FRANK** – you must be up-**FRONT** with your publics. Honesty is not merely an option. It is a requirement. **FOOL AROUND** with this one and you're dead.

» **FORTHRIGHT** – it's your crisis and there's nothing to be gained by denying it. However, being involved in a crisis does not equate with being guilty of something. Denying its existence, however, suggests you have something to cover up. Suspicion is a human emotion. Eliminate it.

» **FOCUS** – stay within the parameters of the subject with which you are dealing. Stay focused. Use a single spokesperson wherever possible. In any case, the company's position must be transmitted through a single message.

» **FACILITY** – whenever possible, utilize a physical control center: a section of corporate headquarters, a hangar, rented hotel space, etc. Provide the media with a place of relevance and control where communication happens and where it should be sought.

» **FEEDBACK** – remember, communication is two-way. Be as committed to listening as you are to talking. The information you gather from **FEEDBACK** may help you modify your program more effectively.

» **FEELING** – where situations call for it – and most will – human, compassionate reaction must be expressed. In almost every crisis situation, there are victims. Sometimes people are killed or hurt; sometimes people lose their jobs or their investments; sometimes people are just saddened or feel threatened. Victims must never be overlooked nor failed to be addressed.

JAMES E. LUKASZEWSKI

The next expert to offer words of welcome wisdom based on years of experience, James Lukaszewski, has had a long and distinguished career in public relations and crisis management. He has handled crisis situations of virtually every kind, written numerous books and articles on crisis management, and has been an advisor to several agencies of the federal government. Here, he writes about a subject that is of major importance to both individuals and organizations concerned about reputation and litigation, both of which can be easily classified as crisis problems.

HOW TO BUILD YOUR REPUTATION DURING LITIGATION AND AVOID CRUMMY TRIAL VISIBILITY – JAMES E. LUKASZEWSKI, APR, FELLOW PRSA, CHAIRMAN, THE LUKASZEWSKI GROUP INC.

Too much public communication during litigation is vacuous, self-serving, and legally insignificant. High-profile litigation, like many other high-profile situations, usually provides a powerful opportunity for those who are prepared to enhance or clarify reputation – especially among key audiences such as employees, allies, investors, customers, even victims.

Instead, we hear legal phrases like: "we're pleased with the direction this trial is taking ..."; "we will vigorously defend our interests ..."; "their arguments are entirely without merit ..."; "these outrageous allegations will be defeated at trial ..."; or "their arguments are not well grounded in fact ..." You get the idea. It's lawyer-to-lawyer button-pushing.

Legal communication strategies can enhance the reputational interests of organizations outside the courtroom if they pass these tests.

» Does the commentary help those who care most about an organization learn more and know more about that organization?
» Does the communication help those who should know about an organization learn more and know more about that organization?
» Does the communication shed some light on, help others better understand, or move the discussion to a more useful, positive, post-settlement/trial/verdict level?

There are failure-prone communication approaches that will probably force extraneous information into the litigation or trial, convince the public of your client's guilt, and reconfirm your adversaries' commitment to defeat you:

» denying the allegations;
» reassuring the public that "it ain't so";
» covering for people who have allegedly done something wrong; and
» characterizing the adversary's position, facts, and arguments in negative ways.

When attorneys speak, they tend to look at all forums as being equal. Attorney commentary has legal significance principally inside the courtroom. Mindless, often negative or combative legalistic communication outside the courtroom leads to uncontrollable perceptions, once unleashed, and serious potential reputational damage when misunderstood.

Judges, the courts, juries, and the legal system are committed to protect the public and advocate for victims. If you're not a victim (and – from the public's perspective – companies and large organizations rarely are), winning the public perception struggle requires an aggressive, positive strategy. Here's how.

» Learn the process and the players:
  » familiarize yourself with the American Bar Association's *Fair Trial and Free Press Standards and Model Rules*, plus state and local rules; and
  » anticipate high-profile variables (i.e. trial consultants, television, lawyers, public demonstrations, third-party experts, leaks, and aggressive prosecution or plaintiff co-operation with the media).
» Encourage prompt settlement:
  » settlement often eliminates or substantially reduces litigation visibility. Settlement sucks out the news value, but builds credibility and admiration; and
  » the check you write today will be the smallest check you will ever write.
» Empathize:
  » negative language, threats, and whining anger juries, empower critics, and induce the media to ask even tougher, more embarrassing questions. Be positive and compassionate. Care.
» Fight nicely and fairly:
  » be relentlessly positive. If you feel and act like a warrior, prepare for, and forecast war, there will be war. Wars are messy, expensive, and create casualties who counter-attack. You take the heaviest casualties. Wars never end. Fire the warrior lawyers, hire the peacemakers. Get on with your life. Control the legally insignificant, mindless litigation commentary and lawyer button-pushing or your adversaries will control your reputation, and perhaps your legal destiny.

FRASER P. SEITEL

People, as well as organizations, can be the victim of crisis, and when you are a public personality, or are forced by circumstances into being one, there are some crisis management points to be known and followed. Fraser Seitel provides that guidance here, using a recent event as the model.

Seitel has been a public relations counselor, teacher, and author for 30 years. His widely-known text, *The Practice of Public Relations*, published by Prentice-Hall, is in its eighth printing and is used in 200 colleges and universities.

PERSONAL PR IN TIME OF CRISIS – FRASER P. SEITEL

Few ordeals are more harrowing than finding yourself alone in the cross-hairs of crisis, abandoned by the organization upon whom you have depended for your entire life. Such was the case with US Navy Commander Scott D. Waddle in February 2001.

On February 9, the USS *Greeneville*, a nuclear-powered attack submarine, commanded by Waddle, set out from Honolulu harbor, with a crew joined by 16 "fat cat" civilian visitors there to observe the Navy's underwater competence as part of the Distinguished Visitors' Program.

At the conclusion of the day-long tour, Cdr Waddle decided to demonstrate to the civilians aboard the sub's rapid surfacing capability. The boat rose quickly, slamming broadside into a defenseless Japanese fishing craft which sank in minutes. Descending with it into the 700 meters of water below were the bodies of nine young Japanese men. And in those few horrible moments, Cdr Waddle's life changed forever.

When the submarine returned to port the next day, the career naval officer was met by, as he put it later, "too many TV crews to count." Cdr Waddle was immediately vilified as the pilot of the killer sub. He was relieved of his command and seemed certain to receive the ultimate naval ignominy, a court martial.

But after two months of intense pressure, the Pentagon decided to punish Cdr Waddle at a disciplinary hearing, known as an "admiral's mast," rather than institute a court martial proceeding. He even received an honorable discharge with a pension.

How Cdr Waddle evaded a court martial and defended himself against an unforgiving military establishment is testimony to adopting an aggressive public relations strategy in the face of powerful public attack.

Step 1 – don't always acquiesce to your employer

Just because you work for a large organization doesn't mean its interests coincide with yours. In crisis, they don't. In this case, the Navy desired that its captain keep quiet and let the official inquiry do the talking.

But Cdr Waddle recognized early that, without telling his own story, he could be getting "set up" to take the blame. So he decided early not only to be visible at the naval court of inquiry hearing, but also to be available to the media. It turned out to be a pivotal decision.

Step 2 – immediately empathize with the victims

The hardest thing to convince any CEO to do is apologize. Even if they are clearly at fault, CEOs, often listening to lawyers' laments about likely liability, keep mum rather than acknowledge their mistakes.

In this case, Cdr Waddle publicly met the captain of the Japanese ship, face-to-face in a court waiting-room, and expressed his "sense of apology for the accident and the loss of life caused by the accident."

Step 3 – enlist third party endorsement

The key to effective crisis communications is getting other, more "objective" parties to speak on your behalf.

Cdr Waddle had his father, a retired officer himself, in attendance every day at the inquiry to meet with the media. Col. Dan Waddle told interviewers: "I am worried that my son will be made a scapegoat in this tragedy. I know he wants to testify about what happened."

In this way, Cdr Waddle was putting the Navy on the defensive and setting himself up as another possible "victim" in a witch-hunt.

Step 4 – portray yourself as a victim

People sympathize with "victims."

Sure enough, when Cdr Waddle made it known that he wanted to testify in his own defense, the Navy court of inquiry denied his request for immunity. If the commander chose to testify – and the Navy urged him not to – anything he said could and would be held against him in a court martial proceeding.

Cdr Waddle testified anyway, admitting "honest errors" and apologizing profusely to the teary-eyed family members of the Japanese men killed.

His vintage performance effectively turned the tables on the Navy, putting it, not him, on the defensive.

Step 5 – use the media to seal the deal

As scary and unpredictable as they are, the media can help turn the tide in a crisis.

A week before the Navy was to render its decision on court martial, Cdr Waddle agreed to sit for an exclusive interview with *Time* magazine.

"I didn't cause the accident. I gave the orders that resulted in the accident. And I take full responsibility. I would give my life if it meant one of those nine lives could be brought back," he told *Time*. News wires reported the interview, and support swelled for the defrocked commander.

Consequently, in the end, the Navy had little choice but to let this sympathetic figure down gently.

SUMMARY

A final word (or, actually, words) on these points of wisdom: pay attention to them; if ignored, there will be a cost.

Resources

Where to find out more about crisis management, receive training in it, and learn the names of consultants in the field.

The resources available to anyone wanting to access helpful information on the subject of crisis management are plentiful and come in a wide variety of forms. What is presented in this chapter is general information that can be accessed from several sources, including professional memberships and directories that include companies involved in crisis management, books of a recent vintage on the subject, current articles, and Websites.

MEMBERSHIPS AND DIRECTORIES

The Public Relations Society of America

Across the US there are several public relations organizations on both a state-wide and city basis. Sometimes these regional groups are independent and sometimes they are part of the Public Relations Society of America. The latter group is the largest in terms of public relations memberships and many companies and individuals in it are heavily, if not exclusively, engaged in crisis management activities, either for companies where they serve in executive capacities or with public relations firms where they represent client organizations. The Society is located at: 33 Irving Place, New York, NY, 10003-2376; telephone: 212-995-2230.

The reader is cautioned that not all crisis management experts are in the public relations business and therefore are not necessarily members of any public relations organization. Increasingly, other types of companies, including those which have been in the past considered as general management consultants, have entered the field, although it is difficult to provide specifics as to their continuing activities.

J.R. O'Dwyer Co. Inc.

The public relations field, like most others, has a list of those who are active in it. There are two lists that are published by J.R. O'Dwyer Co. Inc., which the reader will find helpful: *O'Dwyer's Directory of Public Relations Executives* and *O'Dwyer's Directory of Public Relations Firms*.

The first provides information on public relations people and departments, which work primarily on large corporate staffs. The second provides a lot of data on public relations firms and what they do, and includes a list of the executives in those agencies.

Anyone interested in obtaining additional information about these directories should contact J.R. O'Dwyer Co. Inc. at: 271 Madison Avenue, New York, NY, 10011; telephone: 212–679–2471.

BOOKS

New titles that deal with the issue of crisis management are always being released. Readers are urged to consult their favorite book sources, which will probably include such online lists as Barnes & Noble and Amazon.com for recent releases.

It is well to remember that a considerable amount of information on crisis management is contained in most of the standard texts on public relations. Below are two good public relations texts that are used widely in American colleges and universities. Remember, however, that this does not mean that there aren't a lot of other excellent public relations texts in existence.

» *The Practice of Public Relations*, 8th ed., Fraser P. Seitel, Prentice-Hall, Englewood Cliffs, NJ.
» *Effective Public Relations*, 8th ed., Scott M. Cutlip & Allen H. Center, Prentice-Hall, Englewood Cliffs, NJ.

In a more limited sense, namely with regard to books that deal only with crisis management, the various online lists contain references to many, and more each passing day.

A representative sampling of such books with the very important note, again, that there are many other good ones around, includes the following.

» *Crisis Management: Planning for the Inevitable*, Steven Fink, iUniverse.com Inc., April 2000.
» *Managing Crises Before They Happen: What Every Executive and Manager Needs to Know About Crisis Management*, Ian I. Mitroff & Gus Anagos, AMACOM, October 2000.
» *The PR Crisis Bible: How to Take Charge of the Media When All Hell Breaks Loose*, Robin Cohn, St Martin's Press Inc., October 2000.

» *Harvard Business Review on Crisis Management*, Harvard Business School Publishing, January 2000.

» *Communicating When Your Company is Under Siege: Surviving Public Crisis*, Marion K. Pinsdorf, Fordham University Press, November 1997.

» *The Essential Guide to Managing Corporate Crises: A Step-by-Step Handbook for Surviving Major Catastrophes*, Ian I. Mitroff, Christine M. Pearson, & L. Katharine Harrington, Oxford University Press Inc., March 1996.

» *The Crisis Counselor: A Step-by-Step Guide to Managing a Business Crisis*, Jeffrey R. Caponigro, NTC Publishing Group, November 1999.

» *Crisis Communications: A Casebook Approach*, Kathleen Fearn-Banks, Lawrence Erlbaum Associates Inc., December 1996.

» *Crisis Management: Planning and Media Relations for the Design and Construction Industry*, Janine Reid, Janine Reid Group, John Wiley & Sons Inc., March 2000.

ARTICLES

Another, relatively small, sample of good current articles on crisis management includes as a starter "How to Keep a Crisis From Happening," *Harvard Management Update*, December 2000. Many others are listed in the current texts and other crisis management books as well as on the various Websites.

A number of excellent articles, books, and monographs are available from The Lukaszewski Group Collection, which has a Website that is provided below. A representative group of just some of the highly relevant and useful articles that are listed in that collection are shown below.

» *Preparing Your Company for Terrorist Attack* – this document provides excellent insights regarding what to do when hit by terrorists, an ever-increasing threat (5pp.).

» *Surviving 60 Minutes and the Other News Magazine Shows* – dealing with this brand of modern journalism requires some specialized knowledge. This article provides valuable information on what to do and what needs to be known about this environment (16pp.).

» *Working Through Embarrassing Revelations: How to Manage the Operational Changes Required and the Enormous Visibility* – a lot of highly unpleasant things can happen to a company and they will usually happen as a surprise. This article provides guidance on how to survive those negative events (6pp.).

» *How to Develop the Mind of a Strategist* - a good piece on defining what strategy means and how to use it effectively (12pp.).

» *How to Establish a Professional Relationship with Reporters* - an essential part of crisis management is to get to know the media and how it works. This piece is to be read and followed as an excellent guide (10pp.).

» *Moving Out of the Target Zone: What to Do When the Activists Attack* - companies are an easy and soft target. This article offers valuable help in what to do when the anti-business attacks start (6pp.).

» *Coping with Corporate Campaigns: Patterns of Activist Intrusion* - another very helpful document on combating modern anti-business tactics (16pp.).

» *Corporate Activism on the Internet: Rogue Activist Web Sites* - this threat, as shown in the text, is modern and serious. The article talks about problems and possible answers in a very fluid and developing area of crisis management (8pp.).

» *Current Crisis Communication Issues: Getting Your Boss to Buy Into Crisis Planning; Building a Crisis Response Plan That Works; When to Send Your Boss Out to Meet the Press; Managing the Lawyers; Managing the Violent Threat* - there are five articles contained in this fine monograph with extremely helpful information on each one of the noted subject areas (22pp.).

WEBSITES

The Websites that have been identified for readers here are as follows.

» The Lukaszewski Group Collection, White Plains, NY: www.e911.com

» Another excellent source for crisis management information is Crisis-navigator, which provides current information on the subject and related matters. The service was formed in August 2000, to quote its own published data, "as an Internet guide to crisis management, crisis communications, issues management, risk management, disaster management, and business continuity management." The service can be contacted at: www.crisisnavigator.org

» Another source of information and help within the crisis management discipline is a firm known as the Institute for Crisis Management (ICM), based in Louisville, KY. This organization was formed in 1989 and specializes in crisis communication activities for a wide variety of clients. In addition, ICM maintains a database of over 60,000 articles dealing with crisis and crisis communication which, appropriately, it labels as the ICM Crisis Database.

Among the services offered by ICM, in addition to client counseling and the database, are: crisis research; the creation of appropriate crisis communication plans; spokesperson training; the development of crisis communication workshops; and crisis debriefings for management that are used to assess how a crisis event was handled. ICM also offers a crisis communications course which is held several times a year. The course, actually a full two-day program, has been offered since 1990 and provides "hands-on" training to people who will be expected to manage a crisis. ICM offers an optional third day to those participants who are interested in learning how to effectively face the media, on camera.

Each course is limited to 10 participants. The optional third day is limited to 8. The course is held at ICM's offices in Jeffersonville, IN, across the Ohio River from Louisville.

ICM can be contacted at: www.crisisexperts.com

SUMMARY

Crisis management is a growing and important area of interest and it's getting ever bigger. As that interest continues to grow, the relevant base of information will expand. Such information, however, because of the fast-paced nature of the activity, has a clear tendency to become stale faster, let us say, than does information on a subject such as cost accounting. If you want to stay current, bear that in mind.

06.05.10

Ten Steps to Making it Work

A step-by-step guide to the basics of crisis management, including the essentials of planning and plan execution.

It is possible to manage a crisis without a plan. It is also possible to launch a satellite or to invade another country without a plan. In each example, the chances of success are equally small.

Don't lose sight of what crisis management is all about, in terms of planning for it. Usually, when a crisis happens, it is an unexpected event that must be managed. And, while the crisis is being managed, so also must be the organization that is undergoing siege. As a result, both crisis and regular management are going on concurrently. A good deal of time must be given to the question of who does what.

Crisis management planning, being separate from the general day-to-day operation of an organization, is both special and requires a lot of attention and tender loving care. There must be an initial period of dedicated examination to learn where the organization sits in its particular solar system. A determined effort must be made to identify the primary and secondary audiences that are to be targeted in a crisis.

1. LEARN MORE

Audience or target-group identification involves more than just learning or confirming who they are. In each of them, there are different leaders. It is important to know, before a crisis occurs, how these leaders can most effectively be reached and through what media.

Successful planning also requires an honest assessment of what government agencies, relevant laws, and regulations may impact the organization in a crisis. In short, if somebody, somewhere, claims to have found a rat's head in a package of a company's frozen meat pies, it helps to know which people armed with badges are heading for the plant and what they are going to want.

Another point for some thought is how the organization specifically, and its industry generally, is viewed by the public and the media. Banks, for example, aren't high on anyone's popularity list and neither are insurance companies. Does the organization have a good relationship with the news media? If not, why? If there are problems in these areas before a crisis occurs, they will only get worse before it's over.

How about competitors? Can the same kind of crisis that one company in the industry has suffered hit others? Is there an industry-wide understanding of things that can go wrong? One example of this would be the electric power industry. A crisis caused by a storm that affects one member of that industry, and which creates unhappy customers, often hits others.

Next, good planning requires taking a long, hard look at the organization mission statement. Does it make sense or is it just a lot of unadulterated baloney? A lot of mission statements are simply composed of high-sounding words and phrases. Whenever that's the case, the words and phrases must be changed to be meaningful. If top management resists such changes, the planners are already in deep trouble and should take some time to update and distribute their résumés.

Boil down the fat and get to a specific list of what the company wants to achieve in its stated goals and objectives. And try to be honest. Editors and reporters have a lot of experience and ability to see through corporate mists. They can remember when a company talks long and hard about how it rewards, not punishes, employees who go to the government with complaints. And they can remember how that same company fired the last person who did it.

The self-examination continues, getting ever closer to the heart of the entire exercise. What kind of crisis has the organization experienced in the past? When did it happen? What kind of crisis was it? Was there a crisis management plan? Did it work? What were the ultimate results in terms of the reaction of the public, media, customers, government, etc.? The process continues with an examination of the relevant crisis and crisis management. Regardless of how crisis issues were handled in the past, what kinds of crises could the organization face now?

2. MAKE A LIST

Include every possible crisis, including (but surely not limited to) the following:

» financial scandal;
» physical disaster;
» labor troubles;
» riot;
» foreign site nationalization or expropriation;
» a succession crisis; and
» product-tampering.

Next, look closely at the above list and then carefully identify, within each of the crisis possibilities, the levels of reaction represented in terms of who will be designated to do what and where. And, of course, determine the resources that will be required in each scenario.

In each one of the identified possibilities, there will be varying levels of inherent vulnerabilities, even including organizational survival. Another fact that should surface during this review is that some kinds of crisis may be predictable. This is obviously true in the transportation business but it can be equally the case in other industries.

Once having completed the above analysis, there should be enough valuable material to start creating the crisis management plan.

3. THE PLAN

What is sometimes the most difficult part of the planning process now looms: the development of the actual document that must be followed when a crisis occurs.

It is essential when preparing the document, and when assigning people to carry out tasks in a crisis, that the plan has a degree of flexibility that fits into the organizational culture. One of the hardest things to do when preparing a crisis management plan is to strike a proper balance between inflexibility on the one hand and excessive looseness on the other. Pick the people who are responsible and can act on their own when circumstances may require it. This point is placed at the top of the list because it must permeate the entire planning and execution process.

The document itself, the distribution of which should be limited to those people who will need to use it or will need to know how it works, will contain all of the steps necessary to execute the plan. It should be prepared in loose-leaf form that will allow for easy page changes. Those pages must each be dated and initialed by the people who are authorized to make alterations. There must be one master copy and it should be kept in a place of accessible safety.

Obviously the people who will form the crisis management team must know who they are and what they will be expected to do when the black day arrives. The team must include key members of the organization's regular management group. The size of the team is usually a reflection of the size and complexity of the planning organization. However, in no case should a team be so large as to be unwieldy.

In specific terms of membership composition, there must be at least one person who can speak for the organization without having to call someone higher up for permission. The top public relations executive must be on the team. It also helps to have someone from the law department aboard. Engineering or other technical people are also good additions if those kinds of issues will arise when dealing with the media. If the crisis occurs in a location that is geographically removed from the site of organizational headquarters, at least one senior member from the management at that facility should be a team member. The latter point is of particular importance if there are going to be issues of local culture, contacts, and language.

4. WHO DOES WHAT

Well before the crisis occurs, the roles of each member of the team must be made crystal clear. It is of particular importance that the regular members of top management fully understand what will happen in a crisis. They will continue to manage the organization but the team is going to manage the crisis. And that responsibility must be matched with an appropriate grant of authority. The last point can be a sticky one. There are a lot of examples where large corporations have structured crisis teams and then, when the media arrives, the management either pre-empted the team or, what's worse, left the team with responsibility but took away the authority. That's another thing that a planner must know about the management. If that kind of attitude is present, update the résumé on a daily basis.

Another problem that can arise when some crisis occurs is that the CEO, seeing the cameras and the reporters, suddenly wants to achieve celebrity status. Totally without training, the executive is off and running, motivated by dreams of stardom, a house in Beverly Hills, and a contract with the William Morris Agency. This is not the time to try and become a personality of the stage, screen, and television variety.

The problem, in a crisis, is that the questioning media will often be abrasive, while the top executive is at the same time becoming defensive, if not downright hostile. After all, this person isn't used to being challenged. The result of this horrible mix is guaranteed to make the difficult task of crisis management into one that is overwhelming.

5. AND THE LAWYERS

While it is essential that the law department has a representative on the crisis team, it is equally important that the role of the lawyer be supportive and neither combative nor obstructionist.

Most lawyers will take the position that, somewhere down the line, somebody is going to sue. One early defense in their view is to give out as little information as possible about a potentially damaging problem, to the media or anyone else. A lot of the "no comment" responses that are made to the media are a direct result of this philosophy, which has deep roots in the law department.

And when top management has to make a choice between what its lawyers advise and what the crisis managers say, the former will almost always prevail. The biggest and best thing that crisis managers, before the event, can emphasize to top management is that, despite the lawyers, the media will find someone, possibly inside the organization, who will provide information (correct or not, true or not) during a crisis. The identity of that person will never surface and neither will the motives.

6. MEDIA TRAINING

Having created a team, there is a need to get it trained. Everyone on the team should be trained to meet the media. Even the public relations person should be trained or retrained because there is always the danger that such a person believes they have all of the answers. And that attitude is a guarantee of possible trouble. Training for everyone on the team is available through seminars, courses, and specially designed programs that most large public relations firms will provide on-site. These programs provide a lot of media savvy.

Learning how to deal with the news media during the height of a crisis is not the time to take lessons. Experience is not always the best teacher. The costs in dollar terms for training will be cheap when compared to the costs in possible damage that can be incurred through a poor media-relations performance.

7. PUBLIC RELATIONS EXPERTISE

It is generally true that a large company will have a public relations department and it may also have a public relations firm on retainer. The latter idea is a good one because of the wide range of experience that an outside firm can bring to a problem and because of the ability of the firm to stand apart from some of the internal issues, politics, and personalities that can get in the way of effective crisis management.

If a public relations firm is a good, strong one, and those are absolutely vital credentials, it will not be in fear of, for example, advising a CEO to stay away from the media in those cases where the executive has a poor media-relations history.

8. THE PRESS KIT

It is also important to recognize that what a company makes, or what services it provides, as well as how it markets and distributes such products or services, is not always known to the media, who will descend in large numbers when a crisis occurs.

It should be assumed that the general assignment reporter who covers fires on a regular basis, doesn't have a single clue as to the details of what goes on in a production facility that is busily trying to stop that purple and pink ooze that is crawling along the ground in Nebraska.

The answer, as a starting point, is a press kit which must contain, as a minimum, the following things:

» a copy of the organization's annual report;
» any relevant facilities brochure;
» biographies and photos of top management; and
» the names and numbers of the authorized spokesperson and designees.

The kit should be put together well in advance of any crisis, except, of course, for any information that would be of specific use at a particular production site.

9. THE MEDIA LIST

It helps if there is some information contained in the plan about the media personnel who may cover a crisis. This requires a dedicated and continuing effort to meet the editors and reporters who cover the industry and the geographic area where the company has facilities. For a transportation company such as an airline, the list would concentrate on the national news media, including major TV news organizations and the wire services.

The list of news people must be constantly updated. People change jobs a lot and a list that is not current is virtually useless. Whenever possible, keep track of where people go when those job changes occur, particularly if the move is to another news position.

10. GETTING READY

In some organizations, and this will largely depend on what kind of business is involved, the crisis team may be sent to the site of a disaster at any hour of the day or night. If a company is in that kind of "firehouse" business, it will be necessary to have equipment set aside and ready to go with the team, such as portable faxes, cell phones, tape recorders, pagers, pens, pencils, and a lot of paper.

Crisis management plans can come with a lot of whistles and bells. In some cases, especially those where an organization expects, based on its industry and experience, that a physical disaster is almost a statistical certainty, the whistles and bells are needed. But, for most companies, if the above guidance is followed, the level of preparedness is sufficient.

The danger, once the crisis management plan is written, edited, and approved, is that it will get filed and forgotten. A crisis management plan must be treated just like the ones used in marketing. It has no value if it isn't updated and tested.

Many organizations will test the crisis management plan on a regular basis and that's a really good idea. The military tests its plans, including those for mobilization, a lot. The purpose is to see if there are problems in communication, in people knowing what to do and where to go. The same is true with crisis management plans. Obviously, the crisis management team will not be expected to get out of bed at 3am and get to a waiting airplane, but people on a team should expect to receive telephone calls at any time that will announce a test of the plan.

One of the most important things that such alerts will accomplish is that the people who will need to refer to the plan will have to know where it is.

SUMMARY

The intent of the material presented so far in this chapter is to list the things that must be done before a crisis occurs. Once it does, and whatever it is, there are critical steps, broken down here for the sake of reader guidance, into 10 steps. And here they are.

1. Alert and mobilize the team immediately upon learning of the crisis. Obviously, the team members must be briefed, and that briefing, depending on the type of crisis, can be done at corporate or organizational headquarters, at the site of the crisis, or *en route* to it.
2. Advise the news media that the crisis team is being assembled. At the same time, a news conference may need to be scheduled and the pre-assembled press kits must be prepared for distribution.
3. If possible, set up a media-friendly place for the news conference, complete with telephones, faxes, and a lot of electrical inlets.
4. Involve a third party, if that's possible, and do it as quickly as possible. Remember how well this tactic worked with Johnson & Johnson, Gerber, and Pepsi-Cola. But, be absolutely sure of the facts before getting the government into the picture. If, for example, marbles *did* get into the mashed potatoes *inside* the plant, the word "crisis" may not be sufficiently descriptive.
5. Meanwhile, be sure that there is a clear and written position that is being taken by the company for release to the media.
6. Select one spokesperson to represent the organization. Obviously that person knows beforehand that this day may come and must be ready for it. When it is necessary to meet the news media, this individual must be available. If there is a news conference, the individual must be there and be fully introduced. If it is absolutely necessary, there can be more than one spokesperson, but anyone in the job must report to the same executive to ensure continuity.

7. Keep ahead of the developing story. Anticipate what the media will want and try your hardest to provide it. If something is not available the media must be told why it isn't and, if possible, when it will be. If some information cannot be provided, for whatever good reason, the media should also be told that, but never, never, never, utter those awful words "no comment" because, to a reporter, that is the first sign of a cover-up.

8. Keep the employees informed. Use all possible means to do that, including internal newsletters, newspapers, magazines, and bulletin boards. Whatever works. Employees can be a major asset in reinforcing information given to the public via the news media. It can work the other way, too, so it isn't a good thing when employees have to get information from the radio, television, or newspapers.

9. Follow the rules that include:
   » never lie to the media;
   » never go "off the record;" and
   » never admit fault.

10. When the crisis is over, conduct an immediate review. It must be done fast because successes and mistakes will still be fresh in the minds of everyone concerned. Solicit comments on the job that the crisis team did and on the operation of the plan itself. Read the letters and take the telephone calls, good and bad. Look at every single step. And make the appropriate changes.

KEY LEARNING POINT

Finally, never forget that planning is a continuous process. It begins with analysis, provides assessment of both strengths and vulnerability, and generates operating actions. Once the plan is executed, the operations are evaluated and the cycle begins again. In the execution of a crisis management plan, the test of its effectiveness often occurs in a fast-breaking, heart-thumping environment where the reputation of people, along with that of the organization, is on the line. Mistakes can be as devastating as the crisis itself.

Frequently Asked Questions (FAQs)

Q1: Why be concerned about crisis management?

A: Every organization should keep people informed about a crisis situation. Failure to do so can make the difference between keeping public confidence and suffering severe and long-lasting damage. Refer to Chapter 1 for more information.

Q2: What is crisis management and how does it work?

A: Crisis management includes the planning for, and execution of, those activities that will enable an organization to communicate with the public – generally through the news media – in an effective way. Refer to Chapter 2 for more information.

Q3: How has crisis management developed?

A: Crisis management is part of public relations and its development is directly linked to the rapid dissemination of information by the news media and the obvious allied need for any organization to reach the public with current and accurate information about relevant incidents. Refer to Chapter 3 for more information.

Q4: Can crisis management be helpful in dealing with problems that may arise through the Web?

A: The Web, or Internet, has created new challenges in communicating to customers, the media, shareholders, and others. Proper crisis management planning and effective execution, coupled with creative thinking, can meet (and has met) these challenges. Refer to Chapter 4 for more information.

Q5: Can crisis management be useful in dealing with international business problems?

A: There are no real boundaries that can stop the spread of news, good or bad, around the world. Any organization that may be vulnerable to a risk, such as product contamination or a physical disaster, must be prepared for a crisis. Refer to Chapter 5 for more information.

Q6: What is the place of crisis management and its personnel in structure of most organizations?

A: It depends on the organization's appreciation of the activity, the organization's crisis history, and its vulnerability to crisis. For example, for a chemical or transportation company, crisis management, usually considered as a public relations department responsibility, is a special staff function. Refer to Chapter 6 for more information.

Q7: Are there case examples of how crisis management has worked well and failed?

A: There are many examples of both kinds. Refer to Chapter 7 for more information.

Q8: Who are some of the leaders in the crisis management field and what are their views?

A: Three of the field's well-known and highly-respected members have provided helpful guidance in this book. Refer to Chapter 8 for more information.

Q9: How and where can more information about crisis management be obtained?

A: There are many books, articles, seminars, Websites, periodicals, and organizations that can be contacted or accessed. Refer to Chapter 9 for more information.

Q10: Is there any available checklist for crisis management?

A: A basic guide to crisis management is contained in this book - refer to Chapter 10. However, it is recommended that when dealing with a crisis or preparing for one, experienced people should be brought in for the task.

Index